T2-EVX-975

HOW TO GET RICH

CHARLES R. WHITLOCK

CONTEMPORARY
BOOKS

CHICAGO

Library of Congress Cataloging-in-Publication Data

Whitlock, Charles R.
    How to get rich : includes thirty-five businesses you can start
with a minimal investment / Charles R. Whitlock.
      p.   cm.
    ISBN 0-8092-3983-3 (cloth)
       0-8092-3848-9 (paper)
    1. New business enterprises—United States—Finance.   2. Small
business—United States—Finance.   I. Title.
HG4027.6.W49   1991
658'.1'141—dc20   91-13561
                                                 CIP

Dedicated to my friends,
contemporaries, and the
thousands who attended
my seminars.

Copyright © 1991 by Charles R. Whitlock
All rights reserved
Published by Contemporary Books, Inc.
180 North Michigan Avenue, Chicago, Illinois 60601
Manufactured in the United States of America
International Standard Book Number: 0-8092-3983-3 (cloth)
                                           0-8092-3848-9 (paper)

Contents

PART III: BUSINESS TACTICS

PART I
BUSINESS BASICS

1
Introduction

It is a popular misconception that the essence of innovation is having ideas. An idea is merely the starting point; innovation is about making things happen, which is a great deal more difficult. Ideas have little intrinsic value. Only when they are implemented by determined people may they become influential. An entrepreneur takes a good idea *and* acts upon the idea.

Every day, business ideas are generated by observation—simply by looking for opportunities. Often the key to a great idea is merely being alert and open-minded in your perceptions. Ideas may appear to be revolutionary in scope or seemingly trivial. An example of astute observation was the birth of a water conservation product from someone thoughtfully noting how a glass of water was retained by a baby diaper in a television commercial. Although the polymer that caused the water retention had been used in diapers for years, it took careful observation and a receptive individual to envision what a great water-saving product this could be if it were to be placed *under the soil*. This entrepreneur took the steps necessary to make his idea a reality, thus creating a brand-new industry. (This business opportunity is further discussed in Chapter 17.)

In 1962, when he was one of IBM's stellar salesmen, Ross Perot came up with an idea while sitting at his kitchen table: he proposed that IBM create a computer services division to provide complete computerized solutions to client's business problems, a concept later to be known as facilities management. IBM's management thought the idea was absolutely impractical, so on his thirty-second birthday that same year, Perot founded Electronic Data Systems Corporation (EDS) with $1,000 in initial capital.

Perot built a billion-dollar company using his genius as an entrepreneur and his equalitarian management approach. On Perot's fifty-fourth birthday, General Motors acquired EDS for $2.55 billion in cash and stock, while Perot became GM's largest stockholder and acquired a seat on the board of directors. GM finally bought out Perot's stock for $700 million and a three-year noncompete agreement with EDS.

Neighbors labeled young Thomas Edison a misfit. He was beaten in public by his father, and parents tried to prevent their children from playing with him. At age ten, Tom set up a laboratory in his basement, much to his parents' dismay, since he frequently blew up parts of the house. He went to work in 1859 at the age of twelve. Although he became almost totally deaf as a teenager, he lived what was later to become his motto: "All things come to those who hustle while they wait." There was only slight interest in his first invention, a recorder for congressional hearings. When he was a young telegraph operator, the office manager ordered him to stop using the company's equipment for his experiments, saying that the company wanted operators, not experimenters. Despite these setbacks, Edison continued to dedicate his life to experimentation, stating, "I'll never give up, for I may have a streak of luck before I die."

Even though Edison had already invented the phonograph, his work in the late 1870s on the incandescent light bulb drew little support. His backers were worried about the project, saying that the idea of a light bulb was not new, that Edison was careless with money and already many months past his project deadline of six weeks, and that the idea was doomed to fail.

Warren Avis was told that his airport car rental idea would never work. Business associates told him that such a national business would be uncontrollable. Business travelers would not use his rental cars. The cost of buying and maintaining cars would break him—if he had any cars left after the auto thieves were through with him. There were naysayers everywhere. Thanks to his persistence—and Doyle, Dane, Bernbach's brilliant "We're Number Two" advertising campaign—Avis is now a household word.

Even Conrad Hilton had to constantly fight with his board of directors, who thought he was too daring. Hilton had begun his love affair with the hotel business after buying and renovating his first hotel in 1919 in Cisco, Texas. By the mid-1920s, he and partners L. M. Drown and Jay C. Powers had amassed eight hotels in Texas. During the Great Depression he came close to losing everything but somehow managed to survive. It is reported that he was so possessed by the idea of owning New York's Waldorf-Astoria Hotel that he carried a picture of "her" in his wallet for years. His belief was that "man with God's help and personal dedication is capable of anything he can dream." He finally acquired the hotel in 1950. More importantly, this world-famous entrepreneur built one of the most impressive chains of hotels in the world.

The late Ray Kroc, founder of the McDonald's chain and one of the pioneers of franchising, had a sign on the wall behind his desk that read:

> Nothing in the world can take the place of persistence. Talent will not: nothing is more common than unsuccessful men with talent. Genius will not: unrewarded genius is almost a proverb. Education will not: the world is full of educated derelicts. Persistence and determination alone are omnipotent.

I don't know about omnipotence, but after studying the careers of many successful entrepreneurs, I can see why Ray Kroc made this his guiding principle.

People everywhere are constantly searching for new products and new ways of doing things—in manufacturing, services, retailing, management, the arts, economics. In *How to Get Rich*, I will give you countless sound business ideas and show you ways to implement them.

You will find that all of my ideas possess a common thread: you, the entrepreneur, are using *other* people's resources to create wealth. The concept of leverage in real estate is not new. Applying the concept of leverage to other business opportunities is perhaps a little less common. What you will need to contribute is your persistence, determination, energy, and enthusiasm. You will see that you really *can* have prosperity and take control of your life. After you have read this book, assess your talents, training, and resources, and determine which business is best for you.

When I was growing up in Chicago in the fifties and sixties, I frequently wrestled with the issue of "What do I want to do when I grow up?" I knew at that young age that my future happiness hinged on the courses I took in school and the decisions I was making then.

Just imagine how many of us decide when we are twelve to become a police officer, then join the police force at twenty-one only to find that the reality of being a police officer is not what we imagined. Through the eyes of a twelve-year-old, a police officer is respected and leads an adventurous life shooting guns and catching bad guys. In real life, the police officer may find people shooting at him or her. People may even dislike the officer just because of the uniform. The police officer's superiors may be politically motivated, and the caseloads can become so burdensome that many of the real criminals get away. The courts are often lenient with the few criminals who are caught and prosecuted. The pay is poor in many cities, the danger can be great, and divorce among police officers is one of the highest of any profession.

Don't let a twelve-year-old decide your future. Once the family comes along, the bills follow. It's hard to change careers when you are living from paycheck to paycheck. It's hard to start a business when you are working forty to sixty hours a week just to keep your head above water.

CREATING WEALTH

The *American Heritage Dictionary* defines an entrepreneur as "a person who organizes, operates, and assumes the risk for a business venture." My definition of an entrepreneur is someone who has the ability to create wealth.

If you took all of the money from the rich entrepreneurs in our society today and gave it to people who do not know how to create wealth, I suspect the entrepreneurs would have it back in short order. Once you know how to create wealth, you create wealth; that is what you do. The police officer enforces the law, the teacher instructs those needing education, the fire fighter puts out fires, and the wealth creator creates wealth. The police officer, teacher, and fire fighter all have one thing in common: they were trained to do their jobs. Similarly, the entrepreneur must be trained to create wealth.

Let me give you an example of how one wealth creator created millions upon millions of dollars with very little initial working capital.

Sam Gilbert wanted to own shopping centers, high-rise buildings, and industrial parks. Before his death in 1987, he amassed a fortune worth tens of millions of dollars in real estate.

His first acquisition was a one-hundred-eighty-thousand-square-foot building in Los Angeles. He selected the site and asked the owner for a ninety-day option to purchase. The land had been on the market for over one year, and the seller was cooperative. Sam decided to fill the building with law firm tenants and design common conference rooms and law libraries in the building. He selected attorneys because he knew how difficult it was for law firms to relocate: it's expensive and troublesome to notify all of the courts, pack mountains of paperwork, and move years' worth of records. However, Sam realized that attorneys would be willing to relocate as long as they could stay put for a while, so he was determined to put together a fifteen-year lease package that would be too appealing to refuse. Sam also knew that law firms pay astronomical rents because they prefer to be located in prestigious buildings in high-rent areas.

Sam knew that mortgages on office buildings were hard to come by at that time. Los Angeles was overbuilt and had a 20 percent vacancy rate for office space. Contractors were giving one month's rent free for each year of commitment on a lease. They were offering leasehold improvements at the landlord's expense. It was clearly a tenant's market. With such high vacancy rates, office building owners were having a difficult time making their mortgage payments. They were suffering from negative cash flow. Is it any wonder that many office buildings were going into foreclosure or that mortgage companies were gun-shy about new mortgages for office buildings? Sam turned all of these negative market conditions into a win-win situation for everyone.

How did Sam do this? He asked the business managers at law firms all over Los Angeles what their rents were and how many months remained on their existing building leases. He then offered them the same square footage at the same price or less (depending upon their current rent rate and Sam's projected rent rate). Sam knew that they had to rent space somewhere for the next fifteen years. If they agreed to sign a fifteen-year lease, Sam agreed to hold firm their initial rent rate with increases subject only to *actual* maintenance, security, and tax increases; the increases would not be associated with some arbitrary index.

Sam also agreed to give the tenants 50 percent equity (ownership) in the building. Thus, the tenants expensed their rental payments—legitimate business expenses on their taxes—and enjoyed 50 percent of the building's depreciation on their taxes and 50 percent of the appreciation on the building's market value. Depending upon the location and history of occupancy, office buildings had been known to double in value over a period of eight to ten years. So, if the building and land had an initial value of $10 million and the building doubled in value, the tenants acquired a $5 million value simply by paying their rent. Of course, Sam's net worth would increase by $5 million, too, less the landowner's equity.

Typically, Sam gave the landowner what is called a "carryforward" interest in the developed property. For example, if the raw land were worth $500,000 and Sam conveyed a 10 percent interest in the developed project, the landowner would have doubled the value of his or her holding when the building doubled in value, because 10 percent of a completed $20 million building with a $10 million mortgage is worth $1 million, or twice the initial value. By using this method of financing the land acquisition, Sam did not need to come up with cash to buy the raw land.

The mortgage companies, insurance companies, and bankers were willing to give 100 percent construction loans because they were guaranteed 100 percent occupancy for the fifteen-year life of the loan by owner-tenants.

WINNERS ALL

What's the common thread in this business enterprise? *Everybody wins.* The tenant earns ownership by simply paying the rent. The landowner doubles the value of his or her real estate by taking an equity position in the finished development. The mortgage company has a riskless loan. Sam Gilbert made millions by bringing everyone together and by satisfying all of their needs simultaneously.

This entrepreneur went on to acquire shopping centers, gambling casinos, and some of the most prestigious office buildings in Los Angeles. This real estate acquisition concept is just as good today as it was ten years ago.

Entrepreneurship is easy and fun, and it can be your road to financial freedom. To better illustrate my point, let's look at an old folk tale that every child knows. I have renamed the tale "The Stone Soup Marketing Plan."

A hungry soldier traveling through a village in the south of France knocked on countless doors, asking the dwellers to kindly spare a small morsel of food. Repeatedly doors were rudely slammed in his face. No one had time for the poor soldier, and the people resented his intrusion into their homes.

Dejected, the soldier walked to the town square, a small, grass-covered sanctuary in the war-torn town. He removed an old pot from his knapsack, filled it with water from the fountain, and placed it over a small fire that he made from branches of trees and twigs. He placed a stone in the water and began stirring slowly, stopping only on occasion to smell the water and taste it. An elderly couple noticed the soldier and came over to find out what he was doing.

The soldier smiled and replied that he was making a wonderful, tasty soup, but it was lacking a few potatoes. If the couple wanted to contribute the potatoes, the soldier said he would share his soup with them. They agreed and hurried home to fetch the potatoes. Then a young man walking through the cold wind happened by, and the soldier told the inquisitive young man that the soup needed a few carrots. The soldier told the young man that if he wanted to run home for the carrots, he could share in the delicious, hot soup. After only one hour, potatoes, carrots, tomatoes, peppers, and seasonings had been added to the pot. One passing farm worker even added a ham bone. Each person joyously consumed the delightful, hot stone soup.

Sam Gilbert's success reminds me of the stone soup story. Yes, the story is fiction, but the concept isn't. Everyone must win. Isn't that a great way to make a living and amass your fortune?

BE PREPARED

This book tells you about many businesses that are relatively easy to start. They do not require a great deal of initial capital, and by and large they do not require a great deal of training. Keep in mind that you can never know enough about your business. Attend seminars, and go to classes at nearby schools that offer specialized business courses of interest to you. Join professional associations and learn from other members. Visit competitors and ask questions. People are usually complimented when you ask for their advice and counsel.

Take it slowly at first and build your business upon a solid foundation. Be sure to check with your city or county business-licensing department to determine whether a business license is required. If you decide to do business under a name other than your own surname, make sure you file a DBA (Doing Business As) notice with your local newspaper. Check with your lawyer about the legal aspects of your new business. For instance, your company name should be researched to make sure that no one else is using it.

Prepare a business plan before you start. Discuss your business plan with your banker and determine the possibility of obtaining bank loans. Consider selling equity (shares of stock) in your new business to friends, relatives, potential suppliers, and past business associates who trust your work ethics and judgment. Talk with an accountant about setting up ledgers and other financial aspects of managing your business. Taking a little bit of time initially to properly set up your business can save you a lot of time and a lot of money later.

Many of the businesses in *How to Get Rich* I have founded, operated, and sold. For example, I established the security business with no initial working capital. It grew to over nine hundred employees, and I sold it to Bekins Moving and Storage. I started the silver recovery business with an initial investment of less than $500. It grew to a substantial precious-metal recovery business processing over fifty thousand ounces of silver per month. I sold it to a photographic chemical company that was later acquired by Eastman Kodak.

Many of the businesses described in this book are businesses that I invested in or consulted with on a limited basis. Each business offers unique advantages and disadvantages, upside gain potential and downside risks. Each business is suitable to different temperaments, and some require more resources than others. They all require a serious, pragmatic business attitude. You will need to put visors on and ignore the doomsayers, the skeptics, and the overly critical who may have tried some venture ten years ago and failed.

Reading *How to Get Rich* will increase your chances of success, because each of the businesses I have written about can be a prosperous business if capitalized and managed properly. Perseverance must come from you. Belief in your own abilities and determination to succeed are key ingredients. It may not always be easy, but nothing worthwhile ever is. Keep this in mind: financial freedom is a worthwhile objective.

2

Launching Your Business

Once you have decided to start your business, there are several legal forms of ownership that it may take. The option you select depends upon your business purpose, your financing needs, your risks, and other considerations. Before you open your doors, carefully consider the advantages and disadvantages of each in relationship to your new business. Bear in mind that I will be taking a layperson's perspective. I can't stress this enough: you should consult an attorney to discuss the various alternatives.

Your company can take the form of a sole proprietorship, some type of a partnership (limited or general), or a corporation (private or public). Henceforth in this book, the word *company* will refer to any of these legal forms of organization. In certain businesses, those in which there is a vulnerability to personal liability, I will specifically use the word *corporation*, for reasons discussed herein.

THE SOLE PROPRIETORSHIP

The sole proprietorship is the simplest entity to form. If you decide to operate under a name other than your own, you need to file a fictitious business name statement with the proper agency, or you may simply publish the name of your company in a local newspaper as "Doing Business As" (DBA). The length of time the DBA must appear in the newspaper varies from county to county across the United States. You should call your local newspaper to find out the time requirement for your area.

Some cities or municipalities require a business license for you to operate as a company in the area. Call the city business offices to find out whether a license is required.

The sole proprietorship is an entity whose principal is legally liable for all of its transactions. If an individual or another business entity sues your company, you are *personally* liable if the court rules against you. This means that your personal assets could be taken as part of the settlement or judgment. As you would expect, some business activities carry greater risk of lawsuits than others. Since you bear legal liability personally, if you decide to form a company you should seriously consider liability insurance.

Financing a sole proprietorship is relatively straightforward. The capitalization for your company comes from your personal assets or borrowings from a bank or other lender. The control of the financing arrangement is largely in your hands; other than the lender, no one else must give approval.

There are some tax advantages to operating a sole proprietorship. To get specific details on the current tax implications, speak with a certified public accountant. Generally, if you incur a loss (large or small), it can be deducted as a business loss against personal income. The federal government allows business owners to write off losses for a period of three years successively. The government does this as an incentive for us to start new companies, recognizing that some will operate at a loss for more than a year. Even if the loss is small, it reduces the amount of personal income tax to be paid.

A sole proprietorship is inexpensive to launch. Publish the DBA name in the newspaper; pay a licensing fee if required; develop an inexpensive advertising brochure, stationery, and business cards; and you're ready to go. You are the boss and have no staff to pay. Though you can add the staff you need as your business grows, it's always a good idea to avoid unnecessary expense. Don't have a secretary, for example, if you don't need one—use a secretarial service when the need arises. Don't print more brochures than you really think you can use. Don't buy equipment until you know you will have customers to use it for. Just think about what you really need to get started, and buy no more than you need.

Again, the most important consideration in the formation of a sole proprietorship is an assessment of the potential legal liabil-

ity. If you're engaged in a project like manufacturing hypodermic
needles, for example, the potential legal liability may be more
than you want to assume personally. You will probably want to
select another form of ownership.

THE CORPORATION

If the business that you're entering has high risk factors, you
should probably incorporate. If, for example, you are getting into
the security business in which your guards may have confronta-
tions with individuals, or if you are going to manufacture a medical product that could malfunction in spite of your best efforts to
ensure quality, then you would probably be better off forming a
corporation as opposed to using another form of organization for
your company.

The corporation is a separate entity from you personally and is
generally used to shield the personal assets of its shareholders.
It is owned by its shareholders, who contribute capital to the
corporation and elect a board of directors. The corporation has
its own responsibilities and obligations. Whether public or private, it is governed by its board, which elects officers to carry out
the day-to-day business of the operation. The corporation, as a
legal entity, stands between you as an individual with personal
assets, and the obligations and legal responsibilities of the
corporation.

There are generally two instances where the corporate veil can
be pierced, making you personally liable:

1. Fraud—If you act in a manner to defraud the corporation and
   those to whom it has obligations, then you are at risk
   personally due to your actions.
2. Alter ego—If you cause the corporation to act for you as a
   person, as your alter ego, then you are personally liable for
   your actions.

The best way to avoid this liability is to run the corporation
properly. Have monthly board meetings and document the proceedings of the meetings by taking minutes. Elect officers to act
on behalf of the corporation, and make sure that your actions are
in the best interests of the corporation at large.

The corporation fundamentally records its own gains and losses for purposes of income taxes. Unless special arrangements are made, the corporation's experiences with profit or loss have nothing to do with your personal income taxes. The exception is if you file for Subchapter S. This is the type of corporate entity most frequently chosen for incorporating small businesses. This arrangement is known as an S corporation entity. Subchapter S allows you to take the corporation's gains or losses into your personal income tax situation, but you retain the safety of the corporate entity in terms of legal liabilities and corporate obligations. If you are considering forming a corporation, discuss the Subchapter S arrangement with a certified public accountant. Unless the corporation is an S corporation, its financial performance has no effect upon your personal income tax situation, unless, of course, you take a salary, receive dividends, or sell its stock.

Forming a Corporation

The documents required for forming your corporation can be obtained from an attorney. Or you can go directly to the office of the secretary of state for your state and get what you need. You take the following steps:

- *License and fees*—Pay the required franchise and filing fees. Generally, these will amount to less than $500.
- *Business purpose*—Complete a brief form provided by the secretary of state's office. This form describes the purpose of your business.
- *Corporate officers*—When you file, you are required to name the officers of your corporation. There are normally no specific requirements for officers. For example, you could name yourself as president, your spouse as treasurer, and your best friend as secretary. The key is that the officers named act in the best interest of the corporation.

States have different requirements for capitalization, the amount of money that must be invested to start operating the business, so consult your attorney or accountant. Let's assume that a minimum of $1,000 is required to capitalize your corporation. You could issue 10,000 shares of stock at ten cents per share. Or you could issue 1,000 shares at $1 per share.

You also have another alternative: no-par-value stock. This type of stock is issued when you elect to use market value instead of a predetermined face value. An attorney can explain this in detail. The method for determining the value of stock with no par value is: (1) Calculate the value of the assets owned by the corporation; (2) Subtract any liabilities (or obligations) the corporation has assumed; (3) Divide the remaining amount by the number of shares issued. The result is the value per share.

The issuance of "common voting stock" is generally recommended, but you should consult with an attorney about your specific circumstances. There may be reason for you to issue preferred stock (which means that the preferred stockholders are paid dividends before common stockholders), but I have found that common voting stock is generally appropriate.

The corporation has the advantage of letting you sell an interest in the business in order to raise capital without investing your own money. Indeed, you can find investors who have an interest in the success of your business.

Conflict of interest is an important issue to consider. You should not sell an interest in your corporation to anyone who is in a position to take unfair advantage of the ownership—regardless of whether or not a specific person would do such a thing. For example, the chief executive officer of a public corporation could exercise influence over the decision to do business with your company, a decision that could be argued was not in the best interest of the stockholder of the public corporation. The same is true of the directors of public corporations, or even of the purchasing agent in a corporation who would gain personally by owning a part of your business and making decisions for his or her employer to buy from you. Where you suspect there is a possible conflict of interest, consult an attorney.

You can also raise money while retaining control of your business through use of the corporate entity. Let's say you need working capital to get your business launched. A couple of alternatives are available to you. Assume you have made a decision to issue 10,000 shares of stock. Here are just two possibilities:

1. You can sell 5,000 shares at $4 a share, thus raising $20,000 and keeping 50 percent of the stock in your name.
2. You can get investors (friends, relatives, coworkers) to buy 20 percent of no-par-value stock for $10 per share. You raise $20,000 by selling 2,000 shares of stock. You retain 80 percent ownership.

These, of course, are simply a couple of examples. Your stock price will be determined by such variables as actual assets and projected earnings.

Naming Your Corporation

You or your attorney will file the name of your corporation with the secretary of state for your state. If another company is using the name you picked, the secretary of state will notify you so that you can select another name.

Selecting a Board of Directors

You should select a board of directors who are from the particular industry you're in, individuals who can make significant contributions to your business. For example, the director of security for a large hospital in your area can help you gain insight into the security-related needs and concerns of hospitals. Or a manager of the advertising desk for a large newspaper could help you understand the issues of getting advertisers for your magazine.

The point is to select a working board of directors who can, and will, help you. Most people will be flattered to be invited to serve on your board, and if at all possible, they will agree to serve and will work with you to make your business grow.

Going Public

If you start your business as a private corporation and later decide to go public, or if you decide to set up a public corporation at the beginning, consult an attorney. There are many complex issues to be handled, and you will need an expert to help you. To take a corporation public, you generally have to have a minimum of three profitable years in business. Going public will probably cost from $50,000 to $150,000.

Other Needs

To start your corporation, you will need stock certificates, bylaws for the corporation, and a corporate seal. An attorney can help you get these. If you decide to go directly to the office of the secretary of state, find a stationery store that carries a "corporate kit," which usually costs less than $100.

For many of the ideas in this book, you should consider forming a corporation as the legal entity for your business. You'll have the following advantages:

- The corporation as an entity stands between the legal liability and obligations of the corporation and you—except in cases of fraud or use of the corporate entity to serve strictly individual purposes.
- The corporation can be used to raise working capital.
- The shareholders of the corporation can help the business prosper.
- The directors of the corporation can help you develop your business and help the business prosper.

You, of course, have to weigh the merits of the corporation against other alternatives.

THE PARTNERSHIP

To form a partnership, you enter into an agreement with one or more individuals to go forward with the business enterprise. Generally, a partnership is formed so that the resources and abilities of the individuals in the partnership complement each other. One partner may bring financial resources to the arrangement, while the other may bring management talent. It is important to specify in the partnership agreement what the responsibilities of each of the partners will be.

A partnership agreement should be prepared by an attorney to ensure that all elements of the arrangement are in proper order. For example, what if a partner is injured? Can the spouse assume the responsibilities of the injured partner? Or does some other individual assume the responsibilities of the injured partner? A lawyer experienced in partnerships can be of great assistance in planning for such contingencies.

There are some other important characteristics of the partnership that you should understand:

• In most states, one partner is legally liable for the debts and other obligations incurred by another partner. This is even more reason to make sure that the partnership agreement spells out clearly what the responsibilities of each partner are.
• Like a sole proprietor, partners have personal and direct liability for the obligations of the business. There is no entity, as in the case of the corporation, that stands between you and the liabilities of the partnership. Your personal assets are at risk if someone takes legal action against the partnership.
• A partnership is easy to establish and relatively inexpensive to form. The only documents that must be prepared are those constituting the partnership agreement.

Although there are many successful partnerships in operation today, a partnership would have limited application for most of the business possibilities discussed in this book.

Limited Partnership

A limited partnership may be either public or private, but it must have two classes of partners: general and limited:

• *General partner*—The limited partnership has at least one general partner, who has unlimited personal liability for all of the debts and obligations of the partnership. The general partner is responsible for managing the business on behalf of the investors, called limited partners.
• *Limited partners*—The limited partners invest money but have no responsibility for the daily operation of the business. Their only risk is the amount of money they have invested. They have no legal liability as long as they do not interfere with the general partner's management of the business. One of the real

advantages of the limited partnership is that the limited partners, really the investors, don't bother you about how you are running the business.

The role of the general partner is typically to generate the idea, develop the preliminary business plan, and seek the investments of the limited partners. The general partner issues "limited partnership units" and gives limited partners a share of the profits generated by the project, based upon the number of units the limited partners hold. (The units are similar to shares of stock, each designating a value per unit.)

Many different types of business opportunities are appropriate for the limited partnership, such as:

• Research and development projects
• Acquisition of airplanes
• Acquisition of hospital equipment
• Feeding of cattle for market
• Purchase of television stations

The limited partnership is generally used for a single business opportunity, and it should be in writing. It is a good tool for raising money and letting the limited partners (the investors) share in the benefits of additional business activities related to their main business.

The Securities and Exchange Commission is the federal regulator for the sale of limited partnerships. The industry regulator is the National Association of Securities Dealers (NASD) in Washington, D.C. If a large sum of money is to be raised by the limited partnership, a financial brokerage firm can help syndicate the limited partnership and raise the money. The fee is deducted from the cash proceeds and ranges from 10 to 15 percent of the amount raised. If the amount to be raised is under $2 million, the fee could be as high as 20 percent of the amount raised.

The rule of thumb for limited partnerships is that the units are sold in smaller dollar values. For example, $10,000 per limited partnership unit is about the maximum for raising relatively small sums of money. More than $10,000 runs the risk of excluding potential investors. For raising larger sums of money, limited partnerships are typically handled through the brokerage firms in the public arena. The brokerage firm obtains approval from the state corporate commission and sells limited partnership units in the public markets. The brokerage firm, of course, charges a fee for its services.

As mentioned before, limited partnerships can be private or public. In the private arena, they are governed by Regulation D. This regulation stipulates that the total number of limited partners may not exceed thirty-five and that the limited partners must meet the state's qualification requirements. Because qualification requirements vary from state to state, consult an attorney.

The benefits to the general partner and limited partners are that they share in the tax advantages of the investment. They also share in the profits resulting from the project. A limited partnership might be structured as follows:

- Until the original investment is repaid, the general partner gets 1 percent of the profits, and the limited partners receive 99 percent.
- When the original investment has been repaid, the general partner and the limited partners share the profits fifty-fifty.
- When the original investment has been repaid to three times the original amount, the limited partnership is dissolved, and the general partner gets 100 percent of the profits resulting from the project.

This arrangement gives the general partner a couple of advantages:

1. The general partner gives up no equity in the corporation.
2. The general partner pays the investors from the profits generated from the project, as opposed to having to meet fixed payments on a loan regardless of the profitability of the project.

The general partner gives up more profits than if a conventional loan were obtained at a standard rate of interest. The lender, though, would probably require that the individual invest personal funds in the project, whereas the limited partnership does not. And, as mentioned, the limited partners share the risk.

As long as the project runs at a loss, no payment is made to the limited partners. The limited partnership lets you get into business without putting up your own money.

But there's no free lunch. You have to pay something for the arrangement. You must prove that the general partner has a net worth of 15 percent of the amount raised.

General Partnership

The general partnership is an arrangement in which all parties are equal in management responsibilities and in the liabilities of the enterprise. As in the case of other types of partnerships, the partners are personally liable for legal liabilities and other obligations of the partnership; there is no entity separating the individual from the business activities. Each partner has unlimited personal liability for the debts and obligations of the partnership. Also note that if one partner is having personal financial problems, the partnership may be forced to dissolve in order to pay that partner's personal debts.

A general partnership is used when two or more people have a great deal to contribute. The kinds of examples that come to mind include law firms, general contractors, architects, geologists, and subcontractors. In a general partnership, all members contribute funding and share in the distributions of the gain made on various projects and business operations.

With the help of an attorney, carefully construct a general partnership agreement so that it specifically addresses any potential problems. The responsibilities and accountabilities of the partners, the specific terms by which investments will be made, and the basis upon which profits will be distributed must be clearly set forth. If the entity operates under a name other than that of its partners, it should also file a fictitious business name statement.

Well, as I said, I want to simply give you a sense of the alternatives that are available to you. The point is that you can make choices and even use some of the alternatives at the same time. Many of the business ideas that will be discussed in this book call for a corporation or a limited partnership. You, of course, should select the form of ownership that makes the most sense to you, given your personal circumstances. Your decision should be made in conjunction with the advice of an attorney and/or accountant well versed in tax matters.

INSURANCE

Also consider your insurance alternatives before starting your business. A product liability lawsuit, employee injury, auto accident, or equipment theft can put you out of business before you have the chance to succeed.

Insurance is essential. I know how tempting it can be to "go naked," as the expression goes, but please don't do it. During my business career, I have seen employees hit by trains and customers eat toxic products. One of my secretaries had her desk fall on her back while she was moving the desk's typing return. In my security guard business, a guard shot an unarmed man in front of a downtown bank. Insure against catastrophe. You'll rest a lot easier.

Following is a list of types of home-office insurance* that should serve as a *basic* guideline for your new business. The premiums and coverages are average and may not be applicable to your situation or state. You should review your insurance needs with your attorney and/or insurance agent.

Liability Insurance

Covers costs of injuries that occur on your property to business-related visitors.

> *When Needed*: If you ever have delivery people, clients, or customers come to your home.
>
> *Estimated Cost of Average Coverage*: $20 per year for $500,000 coverage (when added as a rider to homeowner's policy).

---

*List © 1990 by *Home-Office Computing* Magazine. Reprinted with permission from "Home Offices Go Naked," by Paul and Sarah Edwards, *Home-Office Computing*, November 1990.

Business-Property Insurance

Protects you from damage or loss to your business property.
> *When Needed*: If you have any equipment in your home office that's used for business purposes.
> *Estimated Cost of Average Coverage*: $50 per year for $5,000 to $7,000 of equipment (as a rider to your homeowner's policy).

Small-Business Insurance

Provides coverage for business losses—including general liability, business interruption and loss of earnings, errors and omissions, and product liability. These policies can be purchased separately as well.
> *When Needed*: If you have more extensive inventory or equipment than you can protect by adding a business endorsement or rider to your homeowner's policy.
> *Estimated Cost of Average Coverage*: $500 per year.

General Liability Insurance

Covers damages from accidents occurring while you are on someone else's property.
> *When Needed*: If you ever do some portion of your work on someone else's premises.
> *Estimated Cost of Average Coverage*: Included as part of small-business insurance; otherwise, about $200 per year.

Special Computer Insurance

Covers damage to your computer hardware, software, and data.
> *When Needed*: When computer-related losses aren't adequately covered under your property or small-business insurance policies.
> *Estimated Cost of Average Coverage*: $89 per year for $5,000 to $8,000; $109 per year for $8,000 to $11,000; $129 per year for $11,000 to $14,000.

Malpractice, Errors and Omissions, or Product Liability Insurance

Insures against claims or damages that arise out of the services or products you offer.

When Needed: If your work—such as tax preparation—could inadvertently inflict an injury or loss on your clients or customers.

Estimated Cost of Average Coverage: Comes with small-business insurance: minimum premium approximately $500.

Health Insurance

Covers cost of illness or injury.

When Needed: Everyone needs health insurance.

Estimated Cost of Average Coverage: Premium is based on your age, the condition of your body, where you live, and whether your plan is group or individual. Blue Cross of California Individual Policy: $250 deductible, $161 per month; $500 deductible, $124 per month; $1,000 deductible, $79 per month; $2,000 deductible, $67 per month.

Disability Insurance

Protects you from loss of income when you are unable to work due to illness or injury.

When Needed: If your savings aren't sufficient to carry you for an extended period of time, should illness or injury prevent you from conducting business.

Estimated Cost of Average Coverage: Based on age, income, and state of health. If you earn $35,000 per year and the policy pays $2,000 per month after ninety days: $682 per year. If you earn $100,000 per year and the policy pays $5,000 per month: $1,562 per year.

Workers' Compensation Insurance

Compensates you for costs of work-related injuries and time off the job.

When Needed: Available primarily for employees, but if you're incorporated, you can get this insurance for yourself. State regulations vary. May be called state disability insurance.

Estimated Cost of Average Coverage: Bare-bones coverage is about $200 per year.

Auto-Related Insurance

Covers loss of business property in your car and costs of accidents when you or someone on your behalf is driving your car for business purposes.

When Needed: If you use your car for business purposes other than driving to and from work, especially if you transport equipment or merchandise in your car.

Estimated Cost of Average Coverage: $1,600 per year (includes regular accident coverage).

Partnership Insurance

Protects you against suits arising from the actions of any partners in your business.

When Needed: If you have partners or do joint ventures.

Estimated Cost of Average Coverage: A $500 fidelity bond.

BUSINESS PLAN

Every business should start with a business plan. A business plan is like a road map. It should tell you where you are and how you are going to get to your destination. It is difficult to achieve goals if you have not established them, so begin by putting your goals and objectives in writing. Continue to refine and massage them until they are concrete and measurable.

Your business plan should include the following:

- Description of your business
- Legal structure
- Products or services
- Potential market

- Marketing plan (competition, pricing, industry trends, advertising)
- Location of business
- Capital requirements
- How you intend to raise capital
- Financial projections—when the company will be profitable
- Management
- Personnel requirements
- Insurance and security requirements
- Resumes of you and any other key employees
- Obstacles to your entry into the marketplace
- How you intend to overcome obstacles
- Any legal documents, existing contracts, credit reports, and other supporting documents

Whether you are going to the Small Business Administration (SBA) for a government-guaranteed loan or to your local banker, the lender will want to see your business plan. Potential stockholders will want to know as much about your business as they can in order to decide whether they want to invest or how much to invest. They will be especially interested in your qualifications to manage such a business and whether or not you will be adequately capitalized.

If you are undercapitalized and must sell more stock later, you will dilute your shareholders' equity, and they may not like that. For example, if a corporation has issued 1,000 shares and I own 100 shares, I own 10 percent of the corporation. If the corporation sells another 1,000 shares later, for a total of 2,000 shares issued, and I still have my original 100 shares, my equity in the corporation has been reduced from 10 percent to 5 percent.

Your financial projections should be as accurate as possible. Confer with an accountant. If necessary, have your accountant prepare these figures for you. It's critical that you be realistic in your assumptions. Be conservative in projecting sales and entry into the marketplace. If you are not completely certain about your capital requirements, err on the side of overestimation. It is difficult—sometimes impossible—to go back to your initial investors and ask for more money. They may tell you that you underestimated your capital needs once before, so how do they know that you are not underestimating your capital needs again?

More than one businessperson has worked up a complete business plan only to abandon the project. It is better to abandon a project after a month's investigative work than to watch your dream collapse after investing your life's savings.

While there are many good books written on how to write a business plan, I recommend *Entrepreneur* magazine's "Developing a Business Plan." You can order a copy by calling (800) 421-2300 (in California, [800] 352-7449) or writing to:

Entrepreneur Magazine
Order Dept.
2392 Morse Ave.
P.O. Box 19787
Irvine, CA 92713-9438

Whether or not you seek loans or investors' money, you should write a business plan for your new venture. You would not build a house without an architectural plan; why start a business without a solid business plan? Surprisingly enough, many people do exactly that, and that is why many businesses fail. *Good planning*, along with a good product or service, sufficient working capital, good management, hard work, and perseverance are the keys to a successful and profitable business. Finally, you must believe in your heart and mind that *you will succeed.*

3

Salesmanship

Enthusiasm, good management skills, and adequate capital coupled with determination will improve your chances for business success. One essential skill you should develop or improve is your sales ability. Your ability to persuade will help you convince potential investors to give you the precious working capital you need. Good salesmanship will enable you to sell your products and/or services to your customers. Whether you are selling your employees on working harder, your suppliers on giving you better prices, or your customers on buying more product, you need to understand the basic selling elements of probing, presentation, handling objections, and closing.

PROBING

The probing element is the fact-gathering process. A salesperson uses probing techniques to determine the prospect's needs and desires. If, for example, you were selling a restaurant owner on a dinner delivery service, you would want to know if his business is doing well or poorly at that time. If business is slow, he will probably be more receptive to your home delivery concept. You will want to know which charge cards he accepts, how much he spends on advertising, if he serves lunches *and* dinners, if he has takeout capabilities, and so on. The answers to these questions will help you to make the proper presentation. If you have determined that he is not advertising, you probably will not make a big issue about cooperative advertising.

The more you know about your prospective customer, the better presentation you will be able to make. A good real estate salesperson will inquire about the number of children in a

family, income, creditworthiness, occupation, and other pertinent information before recommending homes. Why show someone with six children and a $50,000 family income a $700,000 two-
bedroom town house in Manhattan? Ask questions and find out
what your prospect wants and what your prospect can afford.

For you to make a sale, your prospect must have a desire or
need for your product or service and the ability to buy your
product or service. Many salespeople have spent inordinate
amounts of time with a prospect, only to determine that he or
she does not qualify, so find out during the probing process
whether your prospect has enough financial resources *to make the
purchase.* If you determine that he or she doesn't, move on to a
prospect who does. Your time is valuable, and you need to make
presentations to qualified buyers, not unqualified buyers.

PRESENTATION

The next sales element is the presentation. Use audiovisual aids,
photographs, testimonials, charts, graphs, brochures, and product demonstrations if applicable. If, for example, you are selling
security guard services to hospital administrators, a four- to six-
minute videotape showing your well-dressed guards at work and
interviews with hospital administrators would be a great sales
tool. Get testimonial letters from satisfied customers to prove
how great your service is.

If you are going to use independent sales representatives, you
should design a brochure that tells your story the way *you* want it
told. Your representative can follow the points in your brochure,
and you will know that the same consistent presentation is being
made each and every time.

Present your ideas concisely and with enthusiasm. Present your
products and/or services with one hundred percent commitment.

Always present the *benefits* of ownership or participation. If
people bought products for features alone, owning a Mercedes
Benz or Jaguar or BMW would be just like owning a Ford or
Chevrolet. Mercedes Benz, Jaguars, and BMWs have four wheels,
one engine, and a steering wheel just like Chevrolets and Fords.

People buy benefits. For example, if a car is painted black, a feature of that car is black paint. A good salesperson would turn that feature into a benefit. The salesperson would point out that because you picked black as your exterior color, dirt will not show up as easily. Also, because black paint is a consumer favorite, your resale value will be much greater. People buy benefits, so you sell benefits.

Try to make your presentation to the decision makers. According to the March 1988 issue of *American Salesman*, McGraw-Hill Research's Laboratory of Advertising Performance found that, during a two-month period, salespeople contacted only 9.7 percent of the managers who made buying decisions. If you're making a presentation to two restaurant owners/partners, make your presentation to both at the same time. If you are selling a program to a married couple, try to make your presentation to both spouses. By having both decision makers there during your presentation, you will be able to respond to any and all objections that either may voice.

If only one of them is present and the other one has an objection, the partner you made the presentation to won't always recall your answer. Worse yet, maybe you did not deal with the issue at all. You probably stand a good chance of losing the sale; once someone decides not to do something, it is very difficult to get that person to change his or her mind.

Almost as difficult is increasing the price of something after a price has been agreed upon. Remember: it is easier to come down in price than to go up. So don't underprice yourself going in. Always present your highest price when making your initial presentation.

Ask your prospect for fifteen minutes of uninterrupted time. Then make your presentation.

HANDLING OBJECTIONS

There are always reasons why someone should not buy something. Perhaps it costs too much, this is not a convenient time, we already have something like it . . . the objections go on ad infinitum.

Do not ignore such objections, minimize them, or dismiss them as unimportant. Thank your prospect for bringing her concerns to your attention. Never tell the prospect that she is wrong, misinformed, or doesn't understand. All of these responses are negative and can be offensive. Compliment your prospect's intelligence by acknowledging her specific objection, then respond with your point of view. For example, if you said, "I don't need this book because its contents could be found in ten other books," I would agree that much of what is in this book could possibly be found in ten other books. By saying that, I am acknowledging your point and complimenting your intelligence. I would then suggest that getting all the information you need in one book would save you a lot of reading time and expense. Thus, whenever handling objections, acknowledge your prospect's idea first, then counter with your point of view.

The number one objection that most of us use is the price tag: "It costs too much, and I cannot afford it." You would acknowledge that the price is perhaps on the high side, and you might even thank your prospect for bringing it up because it gives you the opportunity to address that concern. Then you would remind your prospect that we get what we pay for. Better products require more expensive components, engineering, and labor. Would you rather buy an inexpensive watch every year or one good one that may last a lifetime? Support your pricing structure by giving examples of relative value. If a product costs twice as much but lasts five times longer than another product, the consumer will ultimately save a great deal of money.

CLOSING

After probing, presentation, and handling objections, there is only one element left—the order. To get the order, there are hundreds of closing techniques. The most effective ones are the concession close, the alternative close, the urgency close, the direct close, and the puppy dog close. On rare occasions, I have also been known to use the fear factor close.

The Concession Close

The concession close is a very effective technique because it gives your prospect the feeling that you are giving him or her a special deal. We all enjoy a bargain. If you are selling security guard services, you might consider fixing your hourly rates for one year or even two years in exchange for a one-year or two-year commitment. If you were selling your janitorial services to a maker of gold jewelry, you might want to consider offering to replace the carpet you pull up at your expense.

Tie the special offer to a fast decision. For example, tell your prospect that your concession is only good for a few days or a week.

The Alternative Close

According to an old sales adage, if you can get someone to say yes three times, you have a guaranteed sale. If you were a retail clerk and you asked whether your potential customer wanted to use his Visa or MasterCard, then whether he wanted delivery on Monday or Tuesday, and finally whether he wanted the item gift wrapped or just shipped in a standard box, and each time you got a positive response, the sale is near certain.

Offer choices that require commitment. "Do you want valet service to begin on Friday or Saturday?" "Do you want armed or unarmed guards?" "Do you want to list your home with the kitchen appliances or without?" When you ask for the order or special supplier terms or the investor's money and hear three yeses, you will probably hear one more, all-important "Yes!"

The Urgency Close

You have probably heard the urgency close many times. "Buy today because our prices are going up tomorrow." "We are running out of inventory, so buy now!" "If you do not buy auto insurance today, it may be too late to buy it tomorrow." "Crime is up in your neighborhood, so do not be the next victim! Buy our burglar alarm now." Occasionally some of these propositions are imaginary on the part of the seller. Generally there are elements of truth in all of them.

Surely your prices *will* go up from time to time. Give your existing and new customers the opportunity to buy now before they do. Customers will appreciate the lower price, and you will appreciate the business.

The Direct Close

Ask for the order. If you have determined a need and the prospect is qualified, simply ask for the order. "With your permission, I would like to start your service at midnight tonight," or, "Approve this agreement, and I will leave the water softener with you today."

Refer to contracts as agreements, and ask for approval or authorization to ship. Never ask for a signature, because we humans get nervous when asked to sign contracts. Sometimes the best closing technique is to simply assume the order. Fill out your order blank in front of the prospect. Ask for his or her authorization to ship your product, and you've just made a direct-close sale. Pretty easy, huh?

The Puppy Dog Close

Let your potential customer have your product for a few days or use your service for a while with the agreement that you'll pick up your product or stop providing the service if he or she doesn't buy. The concept is, of course, that the prospect is going to fall in love with your product or service and decide to pay for it rather than give it back.

This is a great closing technique for products that make a prospect's burdens easier to manage. For example, if you allowed a janitorial worker to use a vacuum cleaner that was superior to other vacuum cleaners in terms of its ability to remove dirt from carpeting without a lot of physical exertion, the owner of the janitorial service might find it a bit difficult to return it to you. Make the prospect fall in love with your product or service, then give the puppy dog close: buy it or give it back.

Warning: This closing technique is not recommended for use on people with violent personalities.

The Fear Factor Close

"If you don't buy my water purifier, you will die from bacteria or zinc poisoning or God knows what." "If you don't buy life insurance and you die in a plane crash tomorrow, your wife will be left penniless." One salesman in San Francisco sold thousands of survival kits to fearful San Francisco residents after the 1989 earthquake.

The fear factor close is very powerful because you play on people's insecurities, uncertainties, and fears. We all want money in the bank when financial reverses occur. We want adequate insurance when medical trauma happens. We want products and services that minimize our risks and increase our chances to survive and prosper. If the fear factor close fits what you are selling, use it.

There is no law that says you can use only one closing technique. I usually go from closing technique to closing technique until one works.

PERSONALITY AND SELLING

The study of human nature is too complex to be covered in any depth in this chapter. However, assessing the personality and style of each prospect is a critical part of a successful sale. Many sales philosophies exist, and most of us use a variety of approaches with our prospective customers.

You might be interested in reading books on neurolinguistic programming, the art of mirroring your prospect's behaviors. The concept behind the technique is that people feel most comfortable buying from people who are like them. Neurolinguistic programming teaches you how to develop this valuable human skill.

There are hundreds of books on personality assessment that will teach you how to determine a prospect's basic personality. For example, a prospect with the personality of a driver is usually task-oriented and wants everything yesterday. The driver usually hates details. The best closing technique for the driver personality is probably the direct close.

The analytical personality sees most things in black-and-white terms and has little patience with the gray areas. Analytical people respond very well to the concession close and the direct close.

People with an expressive personality have a strong need to know everything so they can express all they know to everyone; they make great teachers, salespeople, and tour guides. They are relatively easy to sell something to. All you have to do is give an expressive person ten reasons to buy from you. Pause for a few seconds and ask the prospect to repeat what you said. After repeating what you said, the prospect will have sold him- or herself! You simply ask for his or her authorization to proceed. The urgency and alternative closing techniques also are very effective with an expressive prospect.

Those with an amiable personality judge themselves by the number of friends they have. Although financial rewards are important to them, nothing is as important as friendship. Develop a friendly relationship with such a prospect by showing interest in his or her hobbies, family, and business. The amiable personality may be a little harder to close than the other personalities, but once you have such a person as a customer, he or she will be very loyal. The amiable person relates best to the puppy dog close and the fear factor close.

CONCLUSION

Whether you are buying a business for little or no money or simply selling a restaurant owner on a dinner delivery service, an understanding of sales techniques will serve you well and give you one more tool in your arsenal of business success weaponry. If you remember and practice the following guidelines, your sales success is almost guaranteed:

- Sell benefits.
- Use testimonial letters where possible.
- Leave a brochure about your business after making a sales call.
- Follow up your sales call with a letter thanking the prospect for his or her time.
- Attempt to close your prospect on the first call, since each subsequent call represents time and money.
- Make presentations to all of the decision makers at the same time whenever possible.
- Present your product with enthusiasm and a hundred percent commitment.
- Do what you say you are going to do.

4

Evaluating a Franchise Opportunity

The ads are everywhere. Buy a mini-doughnut franchise, a quick printing franchise, or a postal service operation. Mobile services are popular, as evidenced by mobile shoe repair franchises and mobile video rental franchises. I've recently seen a franchise for thoroughbred gerbil racing and even one for condom-vending machines. There are hundreds of franchises available . . . for a price.

Initial licensing fees begin as low as several thousand dollars, but franchises are also available for hundreds of thousands of dollars. According to a franchising consulting firm cited in *Sales & Marketing Management* (January 1990), typical franchise fees run from $25,000 to $35,000. According to the Small Business Administration and U.S. Commerce Department, although 24 percent of small businesses fail within the first two years, *less than 5 percent of new franchises fail* every year.

Many buyers of a McDonald's franchise probably thank their lucky stars for their good fortune. Many Holiday Inn franchisees have retired comfortably. Yet there are many franchisees who haven't been successful because they mistakenly selected a franchise that didn't work for them.

Franchising in the United States began in the mid-1800s with the Singer Sewing Machine Company. Now, *Entrepreneur* magazine has reported, more than one-third of all purchases made by American consumers—approximately $600 billion—are from franchises.

Basically, franchising involves "renting" the franchisor's business, name, and expertise. As the franchisee, you pay an initial licensing fee so that you may operate your business under the parent company's name and have the right to sell the parent company's goods or services. You also receive training and knowledge of any special techniques necessary to replicate the business. A franchisee may be required to have a certain amount of capital and be able to prove his or her financial ability to own and operate the franchise. In addition to the initial fee, you usually must pay a certain percentage of your gross sales to the franchisor.

WHY BUY A FRANCHISE?

Undeniably there are a lot of reasons why you might seriously consider buying a franchise. As part of a larger organization, you can .expect training programs, protected territories, purchase discounts, advertising discounts and support, assistance with site selection (very important in a retail business), signage, and, in most cases, a guaranteed business base because of the name recognition of your product or service. People will eat at a Pizza Hut just because the quality of their pizzas is well known and universal, while there may be more hesitation to try the pizza at Jim's Pizza Parlor.

Although initial investment fees may be steeper than what you have originally planned, franchise businesses often are easier to finance than if you were to start a business strictly on your own. This is most likely if you've done your homework, the franchisor has a proven track record of success, and the bank realizes that it will be easier to sell a Pizza Hut franchise than Jim's Pizza Parlor, all other things being equal. The franchising company may also have financing programs available, and because they are securing loans for many franchises, they generally obtain loans at favorable rates.

DO YOUR HOMEWORK

Before you buy a franchise, check out the franchisor carefully. How many years has the company been in business? How many franchises do they have? Where are their existing franchisees located? How are their franchisees doing?

Don't just take a salesperson's word for it! If it all possible, visit the franchise headquarters. Examine their books and records, and find out who the principals are. Ask for the names, addresses, and phone numbers of existing franchises.

Call and visit each of them before making your decision. Find out how they feel about the franchisor. Does the franchisor support them? Do they get adequate training, financing, advertising support, quality products and services? How did the franchisees finance their purchase? How much profit are they making? Is their business growing steadily? If yes, to what do they attribute the growth? If not, why not? If they had it to do over, would they still buy the business today, knowing what they now know?

Call the Better Business Bureau to determine whether or not complaints have been filed against the franchisor. If you can afford to, have the local superior court records checked to see if any major lawsuits have been filed against the franchisor. (Of course, franchisees may have filed lawsuits elsewhere in the country, and you may not know about them.)

Seek the counsel of your accountant and attorney. Have both review the franchise agreement before you sign it. Write into your franchise agreement that the parent company has no civil lawsuits other than those listed on an attachment and that, to the best of the franchisor's representative's knowledge, the firm is not under a grand jury investigation, is not involved in any criminal proceedings, and meets all of the required securities laws and regulations. If you find out later about legal problems that were not disclosed, at least you will be able to prove fraud. Thoroughly researching a franchisor may cost you a little more money and time, but in the long run you will be glad you did your homework.

Do not fall victim to the age-old closing technique that some franchisors use: "We have the world's best location available. But because it's the best, it won't be available more than a few days, so send your deposit in today to hold it." If it gets away from you, don't worry. There will be another one available next week. Take your time and investigate not only the company but the deal itself very carefully. No matter what you find out, at least you will know you will be going into the franchise agreement with your eyes wide open.

PLANNING YOUR FRANCHISE

Be wary of franchises that require a significant cash investment for fees. Although many attractive franchise opportunities may require a sizable initial cash investment, I would be more attracted to an arrangement where the franchisor takes a small fee up front and a percentage thereafter. A franchisor who makes a huge profit going into the partnership may not have as much incentive to help you succeed. I would be more trusting of a relationship that enables the franchisor and franchisee to earn profits together at the same time. No profits, no distributions. Your partner is not the Internal Revenue Service, which always wins, whether you win or lose. A franchisor-franchisee relationship should always be win-win.

If you decide to become a franchisee, chances are you will have to buy the franchisor's products at their prices, which may or may not be competitive. You will have to adhere to their building designs, layout, and operational regulations. These conditions may or may not be acceptable to you. If you prefer structure but do not want to work for someone else, a franchise may work for you.

Your personality and work style should be compatible with the philosophy and goals of the franchisor. If, for instance, you started your own pizza parlor and did really well, you could open additional stores as you wished to do so. If you were a franchisee, you would usually be compelled to purchase more franchises. You will be under the control of the parent company in matters regarding the quality of your products and services, operating standards, location, and appearance of your business. You may also be asked to sign a noncompete agreement for a certain period of time if you terminate the franchise.

If you want to evaluate a variety of franchise business opportunities, attend a business opportunities show. In one day you will be able to go from booth to booth, visiting as many as one hundred franchisors in one location. Call the business exposition producers on the following list for a copy of their schedule of shows. Another excellent source of franchise information is *Entrepreneur* magazine, which regularly features information about franchise opportunities.

PRODUCERS OF FRANCHISE OPPORTUNITY SHOWS

SC Promotions
901 S. Glendale Ave., Ste. 500
Glendale, CA 91205
(818) 500-0005

Spectrum Shows, Inc.
718 Mission Canyon Rd.
Santa Barbara, CA 93105
(805) 563-9118

International Franchise Association
1350 New York Ave., NW, Ste. 900
Washington, DC 20005
(202) 628-8000

Q.M. Marketing, Inc.
Westtown Professional Center
1515 West Chester Pike, Ste. B-2
West Chester, PA 19382-7753
(215) 431-2402

Franchises are normally capital-intensive and require a great deal of due diligence on your part. You can just imagine how much money it takes to build and operate a Pizza Hut, Holiday Inn, Ramada Inn, or a McDonald's restaurant. Imagine the cost for architects, engineers, restaurant equipment, inventory, supplies, furnishings, parking facilities, employees, and all the rest. You may want to consider forming a limited or general partnership to fund your buy-in and spread the risk. Design the partnership so that all of the equity reverts to you after you pay back your limited or general partners two or two and one-half times their initial investments.

In summary, perhaps the best advice I can offer is this: before you purchase a franchise, stop and ask yourself, "What can a franchise do for me that I can't do for myself?"

5

How to Buy an Existing Business
Without Money

Buying an operating company without cash is always a challenging goal. Most of us recognize that there is always a risk-to-reward ratio that must be determined before buying a business. An essential part of the value of a business is based upon a return on investment. If you invest $100,000 and earn $25,000 per year, you have a 25 percent return on your investment. What is your return on investment if you acquire a business without any cash investment whatsoever and earn $25,000 per year? The question almost never comes up. Let's examine a motorcycle tachometer company I purchased in 1981—for zero dollars.

The company had annual sales of $500,000. The prior year, they enjoyed 40 percent pretax profits, or $200,000. They had $150,000 worth of equipment with a $26,000 debt against the equipment. They had accounts receivable (money owed them) of $160,000 and inventory worth $90,000. They leased a 20,000-square-foot industrial building that had three years remaining on a five-year lease. This long-term lease had a five-year renewal provision. As rents for comparable space in the area had almost doubled since the lease was signed, the lease had great value.

The seller wanted $1 million for his business. He was willing to take part of the purchase price in cash and part in the form of a note. The reason many sellers are willing to take paper back on the sale of their business is that they do not want to pay capital gains tax on the entire sales price in one calendar tax year. They usually prefer to receive the money over a period of time so that they pay tax only on the payments received in the years in which they are made.

A simplified version of the company's financial statement looked like this:

Gross sales	$ 500,000
Net profits	$ 200,000
Assets	
Equipment	$ 150,000
Inventory	90,000
Leasehold improvements	12,000
Accounts receivable	160,000
Goodwill*	498,000
Prepaid insurance	18,000
Auto and truck	72,000
	$1,000,000
Liabilities	
Equipment debt	$ 26,000
Accounts payable	32,000
Taxes	9,000
	$ 67,000
Sales price (assets)	$1,000,000
Liabilities	67,000
Actual net worth	$ 933,000

*The extraordinary goodwill value was based upon the company's long-term relationships with its customers and the fact that it had been in business for over forty years. Goodwill is the difference between assets (less liabilities) and the purchase price.

HOW I GOT THE MONEY TO BUY THE BUSINESS

To buy this business, I sold the equipment valued at $150,000 to a leasing company for $100,000 and agreed to lease it back for a monthly fee. Out of the $100,000 payment, I paid the $26,000 loan on the equipment. That gave me a net of $74,000 toward my down payment.

I also arranged a receivables factoring arrangement with a local bank. Under that arrangement, the bank agreed to loan me 80 percent of the outstanding accounts receivable, or $128,000.

I borrowed 50 percent on the value of the inventory, which gave me $45,000.

If you add $74,000, $128,000, and $45,000, you will see that I raised $247,000 toward the purchase price.

I then offered the seller $200,000 cash on closing and a note payable over ten years at $75,000 per year plus 10 percent interest. That gave the seller a payment of $82,500 per year. Of course, all of the financing was based upon the close of the sale.

Remember that the business nets $200,000 per year. With my business and marketing expertise, I felt I could improve upon that profit margin. Even if I did *not* improve the bottom line, there was plenty of money to pay the seller his $82,500 per year, pay the financing debt out of operations, and put $65,000 per year in my pocket. I made $47,000 on the initial purchase transaction, and I owned the business.

Although I actually purchased this business as described, I do not know how often similar buys are available. I do know that if you take the time to thoroughly analyze business opportunities, you, too, can find or create some extraordinary latitude in your purchasing options.

HOW YOU CAN DO IT

While this approach may appear somewhat complicated, it is not as difficult as you may think. Simply look for a business with these characteristics:

- Its sales price is close to the value of its assets.
- It has little debt.
- It has solid, long-term orders to ensure a continued cash flow.
- You feel comfortable running it.

Don't underestimate the importance of your comfort level. If you are not a bookkeeper, you probably should not buy a bookkeeping business. That is not to say that you need to know how to roller-skate to buy a roller-skating rink. But indeed you should be knowledgeable about your new business.

You should require the seller to remain in your employ (without commanding a huge salary) for a period of time after the sale. One to six months is not unreasonable, depending upon the nature of the business. If you just bought a hot dog stand, you may require only a one-day training program. If, on the other hand, you bought a construction company, you may want the previous owner to stay on for at least six months. Negotiate with the previous owner so that he or she either donates the time or works at half his or her prior salary. Only in an extraordinary situation should you pay full salary. Make sure that all mailing lists or trade secrets are your sole property and that you have no contingent liabilities. You will probably want to add a noncompete clause prohibiting the seller from opening a business near yours and becoming your competitor.

One of the advantages in the owner taking back paper is that she will have a vested interest in your success. After all, she wants to be paid her annual payments on time.

When negotiating, be personable and attempt to develop a good relationship with the seller. Who would want to turn a life's work over to someone he or she does not like? You will strike a much better deal if the seller likes you personally. Invite the seller out to dinner, listen carefully, and take his or her concerns seriously. And always remember to dress professionally whenever doing business.

Buying a successful business with the seller's assets is especially challenging and can be very rewarding. Although the numbers and circumstances will change from deal to deal, the basic concept of using the seller's assets will serve you well. Conserve your precious working capital to operate and grow your new business venture.

PART II

WHAT KIND OF BUSINESS?

There are thousands of business opportunities for you to consider. Some—an automobile manufacturing plant, for example—require a great deal of capital. Other business opportunities, such as a carpentry business, may require a great deal of skill. Others, such as a civil engineering business, require a great deal of training. Many businesses require a combination of these assets.

While doing research for this book, I had a basic set of qualifying criteria that had to be met before I would include a business:

- The business had to be in great demand.
- It had to require minimal capital investment but have a great upside earning potential.
- It had to be relatively simple to start and not require a great deal of specialized training or education.

In most cases, the businesses in How to Get Rich meet these goals. In a few instances, such as the private detective business and business brokerage service, I've included business opportunities that require specialized training. These businesses meet the other criteria, however, and I consider the opportunity great enough to warrant the additional effort required to start the business.

I got so excited writing about these businesses that it was all I could do to keep writing and not start one myself! I hope you find the right business opportunity for you to make your career goals a reality.

6

Dinner Delivery Service

With eight million employees and estimated basic sales of $241.3 billion in 1990, the food service industry is one of the largest in the country. However, the mortality rate of restaurants is high. While 12,361 new restaurants opened up in 1987, approximately one-fifth that number failed. One problem inherent in running a restaurant is that its income is in part limited by the number of tables and overall seating capacity.

Upwardly mobile city dwellers, singles, couples where both partners work, and other busy people often cannot find the time or inclination to cook dinner. But sitting at a restaurant can be time-consuming, and many times you just don't feel like going through the dining-out process, especially if you are alone. I can remember having to eat dinner out alone while on business trips. I just sat there feeling sort of awkward. Other folks are busily engaged in conversation, and you just stare out of the window, if there is a window.

How can home-delivery customers who are tired of pizza, fried chicken, and other fast foods, or shut-ins who are unable to frequent restaurants receive freshly cooked salmon, lasagna, couscous, chop suey, barbecued ribs, lemon chicken, or other delights delivered hot to their door? By phoning *your* dinner delivery service!

Home delivery of food is the fastest-growing segment of the off-premises-food category, with sales expected to increase 30 percent annually over the next several years. To start such a business, visit ten to twenty restaurants in your area with a copy of the participating restaurant agreement you and your attorney have drafted. For a nominal $250 annual charge per restaurant, you agree to list the restaurant in your brochure and sell their meals through your delivery service. In addition, you require a 15 percent discount off their published menu prices. Not a bad arrangement for restaurant owners when you consider that they don't have to serve the meal or use table space, and they can now expand their volume without expanding the business's physical size.

You will use the $250 annual fees to pay for warming cabinets, advertising, and other initial expenses. The customer's price is the *published* menu price *plus* a $5 delivery charge per delivery. For a romantic dinner at home or other special occasion, you can provide candlelight, flowers, wine, and gourmet coffee for an additional fee.

Your delivery people will initially work part-time and earn a fee of $2.50 per delivery plus tips. You will also pay them for mileage, since they will be using their own cars. You should provide each delivery person with a name tag to wear during working hours and an identification card to carry in his or her wallet. Although the job itself may not be considered physically strenuous, each driver must be able to lift a portable warming cabinet full of food.

If you've ever used room service in any of the finer hotels, you are probably familiar with one variety of warming cabinet. An insulated, heavy plastic, stackable cabinet frequently used by caterers may be the most appropriate version for you, since it's lightweight and doesn't need electricity. Models manufactured by Cambro will hold food to within five degrees of its original temperature for up to twenty-four hours. Various sizes are available, but you will probably want to inquire of your local restaurant supply firm about those that hold eight meals (approximately $135 each) or twelve meals (approximately $225 each).

Be sure to interview candidates carefully, since these people are representing you to your customers and the rest of the outside world. You will need to get a copy of a valid driver's license and current insurance coverage. Investigate each candidate's driving record thoroughly to ensure that there is not a history of accidents, speeding tickets, driving under the influence, or other problems. Once you have hired a delivery staff, it's a good idea to review the status of each employee's car insurance and driving record at least quarterly.

If your attorney deems it advisable, you may hire delivery people on a *contract basis*. (If you hire full- or part-time employees, you will need to purchase state compensation insurance; withhold appropriate local, state, and federal taxes; contribute toward social security; and provide other benefits that a new business may not be able to support immediately.) Your attorney can prepare an agreement between you and your delivery staff as independent contractors who indemnify you from all liability. Seek advice from your attorney about this, since some states may frown upon this practice due to the tax consequences.

A great potential source of delivery people is senior-citizen centers in your area. Senior citizens are generally reliable, trustworthy, and frequently in need of extra income. Due to the lifting and carrying requirements, they also must be in good physical condition. Another great potential source of delivery people is the local college or university placement office. Students need flexible hours to coincide with their academic pursuits.

Prepare a two-sided, one-color brochure describing your home delivery service. Make sure that you include a few paragraphs emphasizing the benefits of your service, such as fast delivery, warm food, and availability of special orders for special dietary considerations. Since you won't want to have to reprint brochures every time your list of participating restaurants changes, mention that your food is from quality restaurants, but don't use specific names, since participating restaurants will come and go. Ask each restaurant manager to prominently display your brochure. You know that the restaurant patrons already like the food; the next time they want their favorite dish but don't feel like going out, they will call you.

Your printed menus should be reprints of the restaurants' menus. If you are delivering for ten restaurants, you should have a ten-page photocopied menu. In time you'll be able to pare the menus down to the bestselling items from each restaurant and generate a smaller, more efficient menu under your company's name. Distribute your brochure and menus to office buildings, physician's offices, apartment complexes, and industrial plants.

You will need to order business cards and letterhead stationery. Consider ordering printed index cards with your company name and phone number to include with every delivery so that the next time the customer wants to order from you, your number is immediately accessible. One enterprising home delivery service in New Orleans provides its customers with a phone decal listing the phone numbers of the local police, fire department, ambulance, and, of course, *the company's phone number* in larger type. For approximately $130 per thousand decals, it's a small cost to continually remind your customers of your services.

You will want to include your service and phone number in the participating restaurants' ads. (This is an item that could be included in your written agreement with each restaurant.) They are buying advertising space anyway—why not piggyback your business onto their business? After all, you and the restaurant owners are partners.

When receiving your orders, ask for required delivery time and quote the total price, including tax and delivery charges. Ask if the customer will be paying by cash (preferred) or by credit card (use your participating restaurants' bank merchant numbers). Do not accept personal checks unless you know the customer well; if a customer's check bounces, *you* still have to pay the restaurant. Plus, make sure that the delivery person knows how each delivery is to be paid and knows what information is required before accepting personal checks and credit card charges.

Your delivery agent picks up the dinner, places it in a warming cabinet, and delivers it to the customer. The delivery person keeps $2.50 per delivery plus tips and returns the difference to you. Everyone wins: the restaurant has increased its business base; the customer receives a great meal in the comfort of his or her home at a fair price; and you have a successful business with virtually no cash invested.

If you deliver twenty-five meals per evening, at an average cost to the customer of $30 per delivery plus the delivery charge, you will gross $750 per evening for the meals plus $5 per delivery from the delivery charges (or $125). Of the $125, your driver will earn $62.50 plus tips and mileage. You will pocket 15 percent of the $750 ($112.50) plus $62.50 in delivery charges, for a total of $175. That's over $5,000 per month (minus mileage) for selling just twenty-five meals per evening. You should be able to double that number easily. Don't forget: there is nothing to stop you from delivering lunches to offices and industrial plants in the area.

This is a business that you could easily and successfully franchise anywhere in the United States. Your opportunities are endless. And Domino's Pizza thought it had a good idea . . .

RESOURCES

National Restaurant Association
1200 17th St., NW
Washington, DC 20036
(800) 424-5156

Restaurant Business Magazine
633 Third Ave.
New York, NY 10017
(212) 986-4800

Nation's Restaurant News
425 Park Ave.
New York, NY 10022
(212) 371-9400

DINNER DELIVERY SERVICE LAUNCH CHECKLIST

☐ Form company.
☐ Open bank account.
☐ Obtain an IRS tax identification number from your local IRS office.
☐ Order business cards and stationery.
☐ Buy order pads at stationery store.
☐ File DBA.
☐ Check on licensing requirements with city.
☐ Meet with attorney to draft restaurant contract.
☐ Check with insurance agent on insurance coverage.
☐ Sell restaurants on participation.
☐ Have artist lay out brochure or copy menus.
☐ Make up driver ID cards.

☐ Get firm quote on warming cabinets from restaurant supply company.
☐ Call senior-citizen organizations and college placement offices for part-time help.
☐ Check drivers' driving records.
☐ Distribute brochure and/or menus.
☐ Write a business plan. Incorporate the knowledge gained from work accomplished on your checklist.

Note: You will probably not need a sales tax license or permit, because you will be collecting sales tax for the restaurant that already has the required licensure. Call your state board of equalization to verify this, just in case your state is different from most states.

7

Specialty Photography

There are many nonconventional photography businesses that have a compatible customer base. You could create a market niche in glamour photography within existing styling salons and weight-loss centers as well as pet photography in chain pet stores.

The professional portrait segment of the $20 billion photography industry is estimated to be $2.8 billion annually in 1990 with a growth rate of about 4 percent over the previous year. The total industry is expected to grow 5 percent annually over the next five years.

In the United States, there are 32,000 professional portrait studios and one hundred fifteen thousand professional photographers, of which seventy-five thousand are part-time professionals. The average annual gross income for a portrait studio is between $95,000 and $100,000. Sixty-two percent of all households have no professional portraits taken; 24 percent have one or two taken annually. Only 13 percent of the portrait customer market is over the age of twenty-five, according to the 1989 Wolfman report, an annual industry overview.

The industry is extremely fragmented and segmented into school photographers, child photographers, independent photographers, and chain store studio retailers.

To put together your portable portrait photography studio, you'll need to gather the following (or comparable) equipment:

- A Pentax k 1000 camera ($129)
- Bogen 3022 tripod with head ($99)
- Pentax 50 mm lens ($50)
- 2x converter ($35)
- Photogenic 400 pm 104 power pack ($367)

- Two photogenic pm 106 flash heads ($271)
- A forty-two-inch umbrella ($45)
- A reflector posing table ($135)
- A sample portrait preview book ($115)
- Miscellaneous carrying bags

Your total initial investment should be less than $2,000.

Most business owners are looking for additional revenue sources and increased profits. There are approximately one hundred eighty-eight thousand styling salons, weight-loss centers, and retail pet stores in the United States. Collectively these stores generate $33 billion and serve well over one hundred million customers.

Contact the styling salons and weight-loss center owners and suggest that they work with you to offer their customers a cosmetic makeover and portrait photography on their premises. You would set up your portable studio in the back of each store for a two- or three-day period. Each salon owner would invite its customers to receive a cosmetic makeover and photographic portrait for $25, all-inclusive. Not only do you get the free use of the store, but the owner advertises your business for you!

After an initial portrait sitting, you will take ten minutes and offer your customer everything from a life-size portrait for $350 to eight wallet-size photos for an additional $8.95. The salon owner would receive 10 percent of the revenues from any additional photos sold to his or her customers that day.

A related approach is to make a deal with a Mary Kay cosmetic representative to provide the makeup applications, or contact a local department store buyer of a well-known cosmetic line to provide the makeup services. During the makeup application, each would be in an ideal position to sell his or her own line of cosmetics. After the makeover, you take the customer's photo, and everybody wins.

If you have three customers booked each hour for eight hours, you will earn a minimum of $60 per hour if you give the store owner $5 for each photo shoot. Sixty dollars per hour will give you $480 per day. Imagine a $480 per day minimum. If you sell any of your portrait customers additional photos, that daily revenue could grow to $1,000 to $2,000 per day. At $60 per hour minus $15 for film processing, you should net approximately $45 per hour, or $360 per day per store. The customer will enjoy a free makeup application consultation and a relatively inexpensive photo session. The makeup consultant will praise you for delivering receptive prospects all day long. It is just like making stone soup.

Unlike professional photographers, who are trained to adjust lighting, f-stops, and shutter speeds, you will use only one basic pose. After buying your equipment, practice by taking photos of your spouse or friends at different distances with different lighting positions, umbrella angles, and shutter speeds until you are consistently pleased with the quality. Your photo supply store should be able to give you advice on the proper settings, backdrops, lighting, and so forth. In addition, most local libraries have many fine books available on portrait photography.

Your liability should be minimal in this business. Each store owner's liability insurance should cover any contingent liability while you are working in their store, so be sure the owner has adequate insurance coverage. Your attorney should make sure that the formal contract to be signed by each retail store owner addresses this concern. A sole proprietorship, limited partnership, or general partnership will probably be a suitable legal entity to use for this business, but be sure to consult your attorney regarding these matters.

Because you can take your mini–photo studio anywhere, you may want to be on hand at Little League baseball games, high school and college athletic events, square dance contests, dog shows, and other events. Arrange to photograph guests at formal events, proms, and company parties. They are already dressed, and you are in their environment, not a stuffy or intimidating photography studio. While portrait photographers are sitting in their studios waiting for customers to come to them, you will be taking portrait photographs where the customers already are.

In short, your product is a portrait studio that requires only ninety-six square feet of space. It produces easy-to-take quality portraits that are competitive in the market. And targeted prospective businesses can use your business to better serve their customers with an additional revenue-generating service.

You should contact pet stores and grooming service companies to arrange for photo shoots after their customers' pets are cleaned, manicured, and trimmed. What a great, unique service for animal lovers! You should charge more money for pet portraits than human portraits, as in most cases it will take you more time to take pet portraits.

There are many photo-developing stores in most areas. Before you begin your photography career, make an arrangement with one of these stores to process your photos at a reduced rate. Since you are purchasing the film processing for resale, your business will not be obligated to pay the sales tax if you obtain a resale permit from your state board of equalization. You will collect your state's sales tax from your portrait customers. Show the sales tax separately on your customer's receipt so your records will accurately indicate how much to pay your state sales tax collector. Most states require that the sales tax be paid to them quarterly.

RESOURCES

Creations Plus Industries
2804 Marvin Dr.
Carson City, NV 89703

Professional Photographers of America
1090 Executive Way
Des Plaines, IL 60018
(708) 299-8161

Studio Photography Magazine
210 Crossways Park Dr.
Woodbury, NY 11797
(516) 845-2700

SPECIALTY PHOTOGRAPHY BUSINESS
LAUNCH CHECKLIST

☐ Contact attorney to have customer agreement drafted. Discuss the advantages of a sole proprietorship, limited partnership, and general partnership.

☐ Open a bank account.
☐ File DBA if appropriate.
☐ Check on city licensing requirements.
☐ Obtain resale tax permit from state board of equalization.
☐ Obtain IRS tax identification number from IRS office.
☐ Order business cards, stationery, and brochure.
☐ Consider contacting professional portrait photographers in your area about a partnership.
☐ Contact state board of equalization about obtaining a resale tax permit.
☐ Contact local Mary Kay cosmetic consultant and/or cosmetic store owner about participating in a makeover program.
☐ Purchase appropriate photographic equipment and supplies.
☐ Sell styling salons, weight-loss centers, and retail pet stores on concept and participation.
☐ Write a business plan. Incorporate the knowledge gained from work accomplished on your checklist.

8

Specialty Printing

Are you a printer, or do you know someone in the printing business? Even if the answer is no but you enjoy sales and are looking for financial independence, you should seriously consider specialty printing as a money-making venture. Opportunities for you are everywhere. Local maps; opera, concert, and other special-event publications; newsletters; and direct-mail packages are just a few you might explore. I have outlined several specialty printing ideas that can make a great deal of money for an entrepreneur with initiative.

Specialty printing requires no specific training or professional background, although obviously it would be beneficial to have been exposed to the basic elements of the printing industry. Start-up costs are minimal. You'll incur some basic legal expenses to establish the business, draft the few contracts you'll need, and handle any rights and permissions issues that may come up. If you can locate an attorney experienced in publishing or printing, he or she should be able to quickly address your contractual needs. You may also incur nominal charges to buy a mailing list of target accounts. But your overhead costs may be kept very low, since you can work by yourself from your home, and your ongoing costs will generally be limited to phone charges and gas mileage. The main requirement of you is your time and energy.

MAPS

Imagine contracting with a local printer to print your city map. Obtain permission to reprint an existing map, or contact the city planning office for a map-drawing service in your area. On the front side of the map you would place red stars at the locations of advertisers' businesses. The advertising would be printed on the flip side in 2″ × 4″ rectangular spots. The maps would be distributed to real estate offices and perhaps gas stations and restaurants in your city. Large cities might have ten or twenty area maps with ten to fifteen advertisers on each map. As would be expected, this concept will work in cities all over the world.

Each participating advertiser should sign a basic agreement drafted by you and your attorney. This agreement states the fee the advertiser is to pay in exchange for having his or her business starred on the map and his or her advertisement printed on the back. For example, if the ad rate is $500 and you sign ten advertisers, you'd receive gross revenue of $5,000, while fifteen advertisers would bring in $7,500. If you ordered twenty-five hundred maps at fifty cents each, your cost would be $1,250. (Larger quantities will usually result in a lower price per piece, but you may erode your profits by printing more than you need.) You would earn between $3,750 and $6,250, depending on whether you sell ten or fifteen advertisers. To ensure the profitability of your venture, you should negotiate your printing contract and obtain any rights and permissions necessary to print your map before you finalize your ad rates.

A slightly more expensive alternative to the more traditional printing route would be to contact a software company like MAPINFO (200 Broadway, Troy, NY 12180; [800] FAST-MAP). If you have a personal computer and printer, you simply purchase MAPINFO's basic software package for approximately $1,000 and select from their county/street-level map programs the basic maps you need for $225 each. Depending upon the sophistication of your printer, you may or may not require much assistance from your local print shop. For a fee, MAPINFO offers training and ongoing support to their customers.

To keep your start-up costs down, consider ways of becoming a partner with the business that prints your maps. Perhaps the printer will print your first map for no up-front cost to you in exchange for a percentage of equity (say, 25 percent) in your project. You will use your first map to promote the sale of subsequent maps and increase the printer's business.

BUSINESS DIRECTORIES

There are hundreds of specialty printing possibilities, since every industry presents its own unique opportunities. Let me give you another idea. Assume that you are a leasing agent for office space. Compile a list of office buildings in your area. If you live in a big city, divide the city into North, South, East, and West (or whatever specific divisions are already accepted locally). If you live in a smaller city, include office buildings in the entire city. Your list of office buildings should include the square footage of each building, location, access to freeways, parking facilities, special services offered to tenants, security, number of elevators, cost per square foot to rent, and other pertinent information. Local organizations such as commercial real estate firms, the real estate board, the office building owners' associations, and your chamber of commerce can supply this data.

Next, go to each office building manager and propose that he or she buy a one-page ad in your office building directory. Tell the manager that the directory will be distributed to every commercial real estate office in town as well as to the chamber of commerce and local real estate board. When a company is relocating to the area or even within the same area, every real estate agent will have a single source—*your directory*—to use to match the prospective tenants with the available office space.

For each building I envision one full page of written detail with a full-page advertisement directly across from it. Thus, if there are fifty office buildings in your area or city, you would have a one-hundred-page directory. Do not accept partial-page advertisements. Each time an office building manager buys a page, he or she gets the opposing page free. You can charge each building manager $3,000 for a one-page, black-and-white advertisement. If the manager needs to have photography done for an ad, your profit margin should cover this expense. If the manager wants a four-color advertisement, bump the price up to $4,000; the additional $1,000 will cover your photography, color separation, and extra printing costs. The inside front cover, inside back cover, and back cover are premium locations that should sell for an extra $1,000 each. The directory would be in circulation for one

year. Annually on the publishing anniversary date, each advertiser would pay the annual fee—your advertising charge—to stay
in the directory.

I do not believe that any office building manager or owner
could afford *not* to be in your directory. Remember: You are
putting all of his or her competitors' buildings in the directory.
Furthermore, every city in the world with a population over
100,000 can use an office building directory.

If you sell fifty office building managers a $3,000 full-page
advertisement, you will enjoy gross revenues of $150,000 on a
single publication. If you ordered five thousand directories at an
approximate cost of $3 each (includes color separations, layout,
typesetting, and printing), your cost would be $15,000 and you
would earn a gross profit of $135,000.

If you are an apartment leasing agent, is there a special directory opportunity for you? You bet there is. Why not obtain lists of
apartment buildings in your area or city by contacting the local
apartment owners' and managers' associations and the chamber
of commerce. Imagine a four-color, glossy one-hundred-page
apartment directory with a beautiful four-color cover of photos of
some of the most attractive apartment buildings in your city. The
first page in the directory can be a letter from you. You can
address the apartment-living opportunities in your city and
explain the layout of the directory. One suggestion is to divide
your directory by geographic area, so that prospective apartment
dwellers can limit their search to their specific area of interest.

The layout should be consistent throughout, with one page of
information about the apartment complex, listing specific location, the number, type, and size of the units, amenities, furnished versus unfurnished units, swimming pool, Jacuzzi, gym
facilities, proximity to shopping centers, schools, churches, synagogues, child-care centers, banks, grocery stores, and so on.
The adjoining page should be a full-page advertisement for the
apartment complex. The apartment owner pays $3,000 for a
black-and-white advertisement and $4,000 for a four-color adver-
tisement.

Assuming you get fifty apartment building owners to participate, you will earn gross revenues of $150,000 to $200,000 per

directory, depending on whether your customers want four-color. As each apartment owner commits to buy a full-page advertisement, you should find the sales getting easier, since it will become increasingly difficult for each prospective advertiser to say no as his or her competitors are saying yes.

Printing rates may vary considerably from printer to printer as well as regionally, so you'll want to research prospective vendors thoroughly before selecting a printer for your directory. Once you have reached a general oral agreement with your printer, have your lawyer draft a contract incorporating all of the salient points of the printing arrangement.

For purposes of our discussion, however, if you order ten thousand apartment directories, you should be able to pay $3 to $5 per directory (to cover color separations, typesetting, printing, and layout). For a cost of $30,000 to $50,000, your gross profit is $100,000 to $120,000 if all ads are black-and-white, or a gross sale of $150,000 to $170,000 if they are all four-color.

The good news is that you will reap these benefits each year when you reprint the directory: you'll collect the annual advertising fee from those wishing to stay in the directory, add new apartment complexes, and delete those that drop out. Keep your list of potential advertisers up-to-date and stay current with any new building activity taking place in the city.

You will want to distribute the apartment directory to human resources personnel at companies throughout your city, chamber of commerce and real estate offices, and executive relocation firms. Of course; each of your advertisers also should get several hundred copies.

STOCK BUYERS' GUIDES

You could publish a stock buyers' guide. There are thousands of public companies in the United States all vying for investors' dollars. Stock purchases give American companies capital to buy equipment and inventory and to finance research and development. In short, they are the fuel that American industry runs on. Stock prices are, of course, dependent upon earnings, history of growth, and a number of other factors, not the least of which is the emotional or psychological factor. Psychological factors can cause stock prices to rise and fall even though there may be no basis in fact for the swing. News of a takeover may cause the target company's stock price to rise, while news of losing a major legal battle often sends stock prices down.

You might call your guide *The Top* 100, for the stocks included will be considered top selections. Contact the Pacific Stock Exchange in San Francisco or the Midwest Stock Exchange in Chicago for their membership lists. Eventually you can publish guides for the American and New York Stock Exchange companies.

For a sponsor, contact the vice president of marketing or sales manager for the largest stock brokerage firm in your city. Tell this person of your program, and ask the firm to develop a set of criteria and then select the stocks to be included in your book. Criteria for selection should include price-to-earnings ratio, growth, management, new-product introductions, and dividend history. The firm could write an introductory letter in your directory, telling the reader why the companies selected earn the top 100 rating. The fact that one brokerage firm was selected over another will distinguish them as the authority, the source for stock evaluation and investment selection. This stock guide will be a great advertisement for their firm.

Contact the public relations departments of the selected one hundred companies and congratulate each on being chosen for inclusion in the premier issue of your new guide. Tell each firm that the guide will be distributed to all of the stockbrokers in your city. Additional copies may be ordered for direct distribution. Because the company was selected, it will receive a half-page profile in the guide. The guide will describe management biographies, stock prices over the past five years, dividends paid, products manufactured, and services offered. Some of the information in the annual reports will be added to the fact sheet.

To defray the expense of publishing the directory and distribution costs, each company is required to purchase a half-page advertisement and provide camera-ready artwork for the ad, which can include photographs of plants, production lines, products, and/or management. What's important is that the advertisement gives each firm the opportunity to promote the company. Most stock directories are boring and require an analyst's interpretation, so your directory will stand out as a distinctive guide that will be referenced by stockbrokers, analysts, and consumers alike. The booklet should be reviewed by the stock exchange's legal counsel to make sure that it complies with all securities laws and regulations.

You can charge up to $3,000 for each half-page advertisement, your cost dependent upon your geographic area and selection of printer. For purposes of discussion, let's say that the typesetting, layout, and color separations will cost you approximately $300 per page, or $30,000 for a one-hundred-page guide. The printing should run approximately $1 per copy, depending on the quantity ordered. Of course, the more guides you order, the lower your unit cost will be. Assuming you order thirty thousand copies, you can expect to spend approximately $60,000 in total. You can add a few thousand dollars to that total. Each participating company will be required to pay $1,500 with its order, and the balance will be due upon delivery of the guides. If all one hundred companies participate, you'll receive $150,000 in operating capital. Because of the changing nature of the industry, you will need to update the guide at least every six months.

As I mentioned earlier in describing this business opportunity, you can offer stock guides for the top one hundred public companies traded on each stock exchange. You could develop directories for public companies listed over the counter, rather than on the major exchanges, or stock guides for private companies. Another route would be stock guides to specific business categories, such as packaging companies, food suppliers, aerospace companies, the automotive industry, computer companies, or any other growing industry. Why not divide the companies listed on each stock exchange by geographic area and publish stock guides by areas, such as the top 100 stock buys in Miami or New York or Cleveland? This has the potential of being a multimillion-dollar business for an aggressive entrepreneur.

You can produce specialty directories for banks, financial brokerage firms, insurance companies, churches, medical clinics, attorneys and legal service organizations, florists, auto dealers, auto repair shops, resorts, and restaurants. The list is virtually endless and limited only by your imagination.

RESOURCES

Printing Industry of America
100 Dangerfield Rd.
Alexandria, VA 22314
(703) 519-8100

Building Business Magazine
30375 Northwestern Hwy.
Farmington Hills, MI 48334
(313) 737-4477

American Printer Magazine
29 N. Wacker Dr.
Chicago, IL 60606
(312) 726-2802

SPECIALTY PRINTING BUSINESS LAUNCH CHECKLIST

- ☐ Form company or, if you decide to sell stock to raise capital, incorporate.
- ☐ Open bank account.
- ☐ Contact IRS office in your area to obtain an IRS tax identification number.
- ☐ Order business cards and stationery.
- ☐ File DBA if forming a sole proprietorship.
- ☐ Buy order pad at stationery store.
- ☐ Arrange for answering service or buy an answering machine.
- ☐ Obtain business license.
- ☐ Meet with attorney to draft contracts.
- ☐ Call map company resources if map sales are targeted.
- ☐ Contact chamber of commerce for listings.
- ☐ Obtain sales prospect listings from local yellow pages.
- ☐ Contact prospects regarding participation in your map or directory.

☐ Contact the smaller stock exchanges for endorsements, and obtain list of members if producing stock guide.

☐ Contact members of stock exchange by letter and phone to ascertain their level of interest in participating in your guide.

☐ Contact major brokerage firms in your city to determine interest in participating and to draft an introduction to the directory.

☐ Have an artist lay out a mock-up of the proposed directory.

☐ Obtain three competitive printing bids.

☐ Negotiate printing contract and consider making printer your partner or stockholder in your business.

☐ Set up office in your home or in partner's printing facility. You should have a desk, personal computer, file cabinet, fax machine, and answering machine at your disposal.

☐ Consider selling stock to raise working capital.

☐ Write a business plan. Incorporate the knowledge gained from work accomplished on your checklist.

9

Telephone Book Cover

Imagine that you are a retail merchant in an average size town. Suppose you rely heavily upon the yellow pages to bring you new customers. Finally, imagine that you are just one of twenty, thirty, or fifty merchants supplying the same basic product or service. Perhaps you are a pharmacist or own a window-cleaning service or a TV repair shop. How much would you be willing to pay if none of your competitors were allowed to advertise in the same phone book as you? What if you were the only pharmacist or window cleaner or TV repair shop listed under your classification? How much would you pay me if I placed your advertisement on the *front cover* of the telephone books distributed in your area?

By providing inexpensive vinyl telephone book covers silk-screened in one color, you can offer a yellow pages advertiser all of these wonderful advantages. Donnelley Printing started printing telephone books in 1886, and they have not stopped since "Let your fingers do the walking" became a household phrase. If you are a retail merchant or professional, you will probably be unable to resist the advertising offer from the yellow pages representative. Nearly everyone uses the yellow pages.

Most telephone books are approximately 9 inches wide by 11 inches high. The thickness, of course, depends on the size of your community and number of advertisers. The Manhattan directories are close to six inches thick. (Yes, I said directories, since it takes two to cover the Manhattan marketplace.) In Salmon, Idaho, the phone directory, which includes white (subscriber lists) and yellow (advertisers' listings) pages, is little more than ¼ inch thick.

You can fit ten 4½″ × 2″ ads on the front cover and a like number on the back. That will give you a total of twenty 4½″ × 2″

ad spaces to sell. You can sell each of these cover positions for $200 per month, for a total of $4,000 per month, or $48,000 per year. Considering the value of such a cover position, the rate is competitive with those for display ads in the yellow pages.

In each community where you offer a telephone book cover, simply go through the yellow pages and pick the advertisers with the largest display ads in each listed category. Each time you get an advertiser in one category, close out that category, so that each advertiser has category exclusivity. In other words, there will only be one pharmacist, one attorney, one funeral home, one ambulance service, one barber, one beauty shop, and so on. By limiting each category to one advertiser, you give the recipient of the telephone book cover a wide range of services on the cover. Moreover, the advertisers will know that if they do not renew their advertisement next year, a competitor will take their place. That is a strong incentive to keep an advertisement in year after year. It makes the sale a lot easier if each advertiser knows that he or she has the only ad in a business category.

You can buy the blank vinyl covers for fifteen to twenty-five cents each, depending on quantity and thickness of vinyl ordered. For materials, contact a local plastics distributor like Cadillac Plastics (11255 Vanowen St., North Hollywood, CA 91605; [818] 980-0840). The more telephone book covers you produce, the lower your material costs per book will be. Subcontract the printing to a local silk screen shop, which will probably charge you between twenty and thirty cents per cover to print the ads in one color, plus a one-time setup fee of between $65 and $150. If you ordered one thousand covers and amortized the one-time prep charge of $150, you would be paying fifteen cents per cover. If you ordered ten thousand, the amortized one-time cost would be one and one-half cents per cover. The more you order, the more inexpensive the unit cost:

	1,000-Unit Run	10,000-Unit Run
Vinyl covers	.25	.150
Silk screen printing	.20	.150
Prep/setup	.15	.015
Cost per cover	.60	.315

You can reduce your manufacturing cost by setting up your own silk-screening operation. You can silk-screen in your garage or rent a small four-hundred- to six-hundred-square-foot assembly area. A silk screen is a piece of silk stretched across a wooden or metal frame where a photographic image is developed on the surface. The silk screen is hinged to a tabletop. You place the cover under the screen and line it up with a template so each is printed identically. A squeegee is then pulled across the silk screen, with ink in front of the squeegee.

As your sales volume picks up, you can buy powered silk screen machines that will enable you to screen between three hundred and one thousand covers per hour. These machines sell for $2,000 to $5,000, depending on your level of accuracy and volume requirements. When you reach a volume of ten thousand covers per month, you should consider silk-screening them yourself.

You should deliver or mail the telephone book covers to the residents in the advertisers' market area. In addition, you will want to give each advertiser 250 covers. Your advertisers can give covers to their customers as a gift with purchases. Your maximum distribution should be approximately ten thousand covers per area. In a small community with ten thousand population, you would offer only one cover. In a large metropolitan area, you may sell thirty or forty different covers. For example, in the Chicago area, you would have a cover for Arlington Heights, one for Evanston, the Near North Side, the Far North Side, the Near West Side, and so on.

You can buy residential mailing lists from a local list broker. Brokers typically supply lists of names by zip code on pressure-sensitive labels that will cost you approximately $50 to $75 per thousand. If you distribute 250 covers to each advertiser, that totals five thousand covers (20 advertisers times 250 covers each). Then if you mail an additional five thousand copies, you will pay approximately $250 to $375 for the address labels.

You will want to obtain a bulk permit from your local post office to keep your postage below thirty cents in most cases (depending on the final weight of your finished cover). If you add your manufacturing cost, label cost, and postage, your total costs should be under $1 per cover. That will give you a $10,000 cost to produce a $48,000 sale, for a profit of $38,000 per telephone book cover. Ten covers will net you over one quarter of a million dollars per year. Not bad for a garage business.

Advertisers are accustomed to paying on a monthly basis. If you are billing $4,000 per month, you can see that you will need some initial working capital to pay for the raw material, silk-screening, lists, and postage. If you do not have the working capital, there is an alternative: form a corporation and sell stock in your corporation.

You can have your advertisers sign a one-year contract wherein they agree to pay $200 per month. Have the advertiser fill out a credit application. Take the contract and credit application to your banker and borrow 50 percent of the contract's cash value. That would give you a $1,200 cash advance on each contract. Sign eight of the twenty advertisers, and your banker lends you $9,600. That's enough cash to finance your first cover. As the monthly payments come in, start financing the covers out of your own cash flow. No sense paying interest on money you do not need.

RESOURCES

Point of Purchase Advertising Institute
66 N. Van Brunt St.
Englewood, NJ 07631
(201) 894-8899

Step by Step Graphics Magazine
6000 N. Forest Park
Peoria, IL 61614
(309) 688-2300

TELEPHONE BOOK COVER BUSINESS
LAUNCH CHECKLIST

☐ Form a company or corporation.
☐ Open a bank account.
☐ Obtain an IRS tax identification number from IRS office.

☐ Order business cards, stationery, and descriptive brochures.
☐ File a DBA with your local newspaper if appropriate.
☐ Have attorney draft advertising sales contract.
☐ Contact vinyl cover source.
☐ Contact silk screen production shop in your area.
☐ Obtain a bulk permit number from your local post office.
☐ Contact a list broker for a quote for providing you with names by zip code.
☐ Contact banker to set up customer financing.
☐ Obtain business license if required by your city.
☐ Make sales calls on potential advertisers.
☐ Write a business plan. Incorporate the knowledge gained from work accomplished on your checklist.

10

Independent Sales Representative

The average cost of a business-to-business sales call is $239, reports *Sales & Marketing Management* magazine (January 1990). In a survey with Personnel Corporation of America, the magazine found that the overall cost of one sale averages 14.5 percent of a company's total sales volume, but at some businesses it can escalate to as high as 35 percent. This cost includes the salesperson's salary, commissions, benefits, expenses, and administrative support. The survey also reported that to close a first sale requires an average of *seven* calls, while generating sales with established customers requires only three calls.

A great percentage of small to medium-sized companies simply cannot afford to keep salespeople on staff. If they have a product distributed regionally or nationally, their costs go up exponentially in some cases; instead of paying auto expenses, they are buying airline tickets and paying expensive hotel bills. As an alternative, they could hire additional sales staff in other regions or cities, but they'd have to hire sales managers and worry about whether or not calls are being made. I knew one salesman who worked for three companies at the same time. He was actually on three separate payrolls. When he took a customer out to dinner, he submitted the dinner expense to all three companies. All of the companies were in the medical field, but none of them were competing with the others. This guy was the small-business owner's worst nightmare.

Such nightmares are part of the reason that independent sales representatives are in great demand. They pay their own expenses and make nothing unless they sell something. Using independent reps, a small company can afford to have representation in every city in the United States and Canada. If a company pays an independent representative a 20 percent commission, it usually caps its sales expense below that of its competitors and pays only on *results*. I know independent publisher's representatives who earn over $1 million a year selling advertising space in magazines. I knew of one independent manufacturer's representative in Chicago who made over $1 million per year selling electronic components.

If you are in sales now or believe you have good sales potential, this may be the right business for you. It is very easy to get started. First, decide what product or service you want to sell. Pick something that you can get *passionate* about. If you love bicycling, for example, contact the manufacturer of a bicycle you think is better than other bicycles in a similar class. Ask the sales manager if the company has representation in your area. Then ask if the manager would be interested in hiring a sales representative on a straight commission basis. If the answer is yes, you are off to the races!

The same call can be made to manufacturers of every product imaginable. Do you want to sell x-ray machines, television sets, pianos, towels, linen service, advertising, television commercials, or airplanes? Each of these products has independent representatives selling in the marketplace.

I know one salesman who sold remodeling for a construction company. He earned a salary of $4,000 per month and a 1 percent commission on sales. His commission brought him an average of $500 per month. That gave him an average monthly paycheck of $4,500 and an annual salary and commission of approximately $54,000. His employer suddenly filed for bankruptcy, and he was out of a job. At the time his sales manager let him go, the salesman had thirty to forty pending construction jobs ranging in value from $5,000 for a kitchen cabinet installation job to $170,000 for building a guest house on a millionaire's country estate. The salesman contacted two of his old competitors for a job. He was anxious to earn a commission on the many pending jobs that he felt confident he could close.

With time passing and his competitors now hot on the trail of these jobs, he contacted a medium-sized construction company on the other side of town, but it could not afford a salesman; the owner made all of the sales calls. After a brief discussion with the owner, he struck a deal whereby the owner agreed to pay him 20 percent on all sales. The salesman sold eleven of the jobs in the first week. He handed $139,000 worth of business to the owner of the construction company and earned $27,800. He went on to earn over $200,000 in his first year. The salesman wondered why he had not gone into business for himself ten years earlier.

You'll want to open a small office in your home or close to your home, order your stationery and business cards, and set up a bank account. A personal computer would be a real plus in managing your accounts. Talk to your attorney about an agreement between you and the company you want to sell for. You may wish to contact the Manufacturers' Agents National Association for membership information and a copy of its booklet on contractual guidelines. Your sales representative agreement should state that you are a free agent and not an employee. Define your territory well. In some cases it may be all of North America; in other cases it may be a single market segment in one city. You may be able to negotiate reimbursement of your out-of-pocket expenses, but that is very unusual. Make sure that all purchase orders go to you first, so that you will be able to keep track of your sales. Your contract will probably provide for payments to you within thirty days after your client (manufacturer) receives payment from your customer. So make sure you have some operating capital to weather the periods of slow cash flow.

One word of caution. It is not uncommon for independent sales representatives to establish a good money-making territory only to receive a representation termination letter, which is just the opposite of what normally happens when you perform well as a salesperson employed by a company. Once you have developed a territory that's really producing, your client's management may decide to stop paying you $50,000 to $200,000 or more and hire its own salesperson for considerably less money. One way to discourage your client from doing this is to include in your original agreement a termination clause that mandates a six-month extension to your contract for each year of service. If you have been selling for them for five years, they owe you an extension of two and one-half years. That will make it pretty difficult to let you go.

Eventually you can hire salespeople to work for you. Pay them a base salary and 1 percent commission. And by the way—*don't* give them a copy of this book.

RESOURCES

The Manufacturers' Agents National Association
23016 Mill Creek Rd.
Laguna Hills, CA 92653
(714) 859-4040

Sales & Marketing Management Magazine
Bill Communications Inc.
633 Third Ave.
New York, NY 10017
(212) 986-4800

INDEPENDENT SALES REPRESENTATIVE BUSINESS LAUNCH CHECKLIST

☐ Consider forming a corporation.
☐ Open a bank account.
☐ Obtain an IRS tax identification number from IRS office.
☐ Order business cards and stationery.
☐ Contact Manufacturers' Agents National Association for sample client agreement and member benefit information.
☐ Contact insurance agent to obtain auto insurance, health insurance, and other insurance.
☐ File DBA if appropriate.
☐ Contact your city business office to determine whether a city license is required.
☐ Set up an office in your home or close to your home. To start, you will need a desk, file cabinet, fax machine, small personal computer, and printer.
☐ Contact potential manufacturing clients.
☐ Write a business plan. Incorporate the knowledge gained from work accomplished on your checklist.

11

Security Guard

According to an article in *Forbes* (September 17, 1990), the security industry is projected to grow 7 to 10 percent a year for the next several years, as we continue to experience an increase in crime. We *all* become victims of crime. We suffer from the rising insurance rates as insurance companies pay out huge sums of money to cover losses due to theft, damage to property, and physical injuries to people. And we pay increased prices as merchants are forced to cover the costs stemming from shoplifting and employee theft.

One significant deterrent to crime is the uniformed security guard. With greater frequency, department stores and retail shopping malls are using uniformed security guards instead of plainclothes detectives. The uniform warns would-be thieves to stay away. Pinkerton's, Inc., now has thirty-eight thousand guards, fifteen thousand clients, and 208 offices in the United States, Canada, and the United Kingdom. Ninety-eight percent of the firm's revenues (sales in 1989 were $605 million) are from basic physical plant protection. Even in a recession, the security industry does well. The need for security exists in both good and bad economic times.

When I started Whitlock Investigations Corporation, a security guard business, I invested no money personally, and one year later I had almost a thousand guards in southern California. Each security guard was contributing approximately $1 per hour in profit to my savings account. I used to tell attendees at my seminars that the sure way to wealth and financial freedom was to have one thousand employees each contributing $1 per hour to your savings account. That is $24,000 per day, or $168,000 per seven-day week. Remember: security is a twenty-four-hour-per-day, seven-days-a-week proposition. Here is how I did it.

I knew that most security guard companies offer guard services to industrial customers, medical centers, hospitals, construction companies, airports, or wherever the need for security exists. While each potential customer has specialized needs, none of the security companies offered specialized services. An armed guard working at a federal courthouse one week may not be qualified to work at a bank the next week. For example, he might not know that there is fluorescent powder–coated money in the cashiers' drawers. When a robber is caught fleeing the bank, the telltale powder signs will show up on the thief's hands under ultraviolet light. The guard should also know not to attempt to stop the robbery. A shoot-out inside a bank can leave a lot of innocent people injured or dead.

I reasoned that a security guard company that specialized in a particular industry would have a good chance of capturing that segment of business. Banks were a good prospect but required only one guard per branch, and at that time banks were not open long hours in comparison to other businesses. Industrial security offered limited financial inducement, since the usual requirement for security guard service was for nighttime only, and generally one guard at the main gate was sufficient. Moreover, many industrial facilities hired their own security guards. Diligently I worked through the specific opportunities afforded the security guard company and decided to provide specialized guard services for *hospitals*.

To my knowledge no one in southern California was providing a specialized hospital security service. Yet hospitals require security twenty-four hours per day, seven days per week. They are required by law in most states to keep their emergency department doors open twenty-four hours per day and are also required to accept phone calls twenty-four hours per day. In most cases one guard is not sufficient to police all of the patient corridors, support departments, and grounds. The need for security is great: hospitals are staffed primarily with female employees; drugs are readily available, as are valuables such as silver in radiology and safes in the business office; and every-thing a criminal needs to manufacture illegal drugs is sitting in Pathology. The hospital is a target for every criminal element, including rapists, drug pushers, drug users, and petty and pro-fessional thieves.

My first sales presentation was made to the administrator of a Sunland hospital in southern California. The administrator com-plained about other security guards stealing hospital assets. The guards were typically under twenty-one or over sixty-five years of age and lacked any training whatsoever. He complained about guards coming to work under the influence of drugs and alcohol. He stated that he had once hired a security guard company that used trained dogs to accompany guards as they patrolled the hospital perimeter. Unfortunately, one of the dogs couldn't dif-ferentiate between criminals and physicians, and a lawsuit ensued when the dog bit an attending surgeon's leg as he was getting out of his car at one o'clock in the morning.

After listening to the administrator's concerns and obvious frustration, I proposed to him that I would provide security guards who were neatly dressed and trained in martial arts and interpersonal relations. My guards would be sensitive to the nature of the hospital's inner workings, its needs, and its vulner-abilities. In exchange for these highly trained guards I required three basic concessions:

1. The administrator must sign the agreement for guard service immediately for a ninety-day trial period.
2. He would pay $1 an hour more per guard than he was currently paying.
3. He would pay one week in advance immediately and every Friday thereafter.

I think that he was so frustrated that he would have agreed to almost anything, because he readily accepted my terms. While I sat in his office, he phoned the incumbent security guard com-pany's sales representative and terminated their contract on the spot. My contract went into effect at midnight *that night*.

The three-hundred-bed hospital required three security guards per shift, three shifts per day. They had been paying $9 per hour for unarmed security guards. That meant that they were paying $9 per hour for 504 man-hours per week (3 men × 24 hours × 7 days = 504), or $4,536 per week. They would be paying me $504 more ($1 × 3 guards × 24 hours × 7 days = $504), or $5,040 per week. I walked down to the controller's office and picked up my first week's advance payment of $5,040.

I drove to a local police uniform rental store and rented a security guard uniform with badge, gun belt, and flashlight. (I also purchased captain's bars for my collar. What the heck? I was in charge.) I immediately returned to the hospital. I called the state unemployment office and asked them to send security guard employment applicants to the hospital. I interviewed the applicants in the hospital cafeteria, and by the end of the first day I hired Sergeant Chambers, Corporal Hurley, and four security guards. They all had experience, could speak intelligently, and expressed ambition. I was in the security guard business just that fast, and I had not spent one cent of my own money. In fact, I had over $5,000 of my customer's money.

I immediately contacted the American Hospital Association in Chicago to order their manual on hospital security. I asked them to air mail the book so that I could quickly get up to speed on the subject of hospital security.

Upon receipt of the book, I began teaching my guards about hospital security. Twice a week I would hold training classes in the hospital training room. After several months of giving the same lecture, I videotaped the presentation. As new security guards were hired, they viewed the tape and received training specific to the particular hospital to which they'd be assigned. Eventually, I arranged for competitive target contests at a nearby firing range and established a one-page newsletter for distribution to my employees and customers. All guards were required to take a basic martial arts class six hours per month with pay, and I provided four hours per month of training in interpersonal relations.

Much to my surprise, I found out that the State of California, like most other states, requires the owner of a security guard company to be licensed. This procedure requires that the applicant take and pass a written test and not have a felony record.

Fortunately the state was scheduled to administer the test just days after I found out that it was required. I took the examination, passed the criminal background check, submitted my fingerprints, and my license was issued. (I was licensed later under a similar procedure as a private investigator so that I could investigate malpractice cases. See the next chapter entitled "Private Detective Agency.")

Hospitals began coming to me to give me their security contracts. Word spread, and before I knew it I had the majority of the hospitals in southern California and Hawaii under contract. Even small hospitals that had never before used security guards were becoming customers. The law requires that hospitals staff switchboards twenty-four hours per day. I simply trained my guards to answer switchboards or trained the hospital's existing switchboard operators in security. Thus, evening rounds of checking patient rooms and support areas could be made using a mobile phone, and one person could do two jobs.

In one year my little company grew from 1 hospital with 6 guards to 198 hospitals with 994 guards. Most companies can't handle that kind of growth due to the cash flow constraints. Many a company has expanded so fast that it fails because it runs out of cash. For example, imagine that you manufacture widgets. You invest $10,000 to produce the widget, $500 to ship it, and you invoice your customer $20,000. Imagine that your customer doesn't pay for two months. In the meantime, you continue to produce widgets for another customer. Even though you haven't been paid, you still have to pay your payroll, rent, phone, and other overhead costs. If all you had to begin with was $10,500, you would have to lay people off, stop making widgets, and might go out of business even though you have contracts, customers, and a $20,000 receivable. Cash flow is the lifeblood of all business, and without positive cash flow you probably won't be around long.

Remember the third condition that I imposed upon the first and all subsequent administrators: they had to pay me one week *in advance*. I withheld each new guard's first paycheck to get his name and payroll data entered into the computer. He received his first week's check at the end of the second week. He aver-

aged $5 per hour, so he received a gross of $200 ($5 per hour ×
40 hours = $200), while I had received $10,080 ($5,040 × 2
weeks). As the number of guards increased to thirteen and each
received $200, my payroll totaled $2,600, giving me a positive
cash flow of $7,480 for the first two weeks. I did not have to
borrow money or sell stock to raise working capital, because my
customers provided the working capital. This is a great concept
and one worth keeping in mind.

You can specialize in hospital security in your locality, or you
may find better opportunities in your community in other specialty areas such as bank security, special-event security, airport
security, or patrol services for retail merchants. Each offers
exciting challenges and corresponding problems. For instance, a
patrol service would require vehicles that are specially
equipped with radio communications equipment and a staffed
home base receiving system for dispatching vehicles with guards
to emergency call sites. Special-events security requires highly
specialized training in crowd control, riot control, and suspect
analysis.

Security is a profitable and rewarding business. The turnover
of employees is comparatively high. The hours are typically long,
and the problems are many. One inherent problem is the mental,
emotional, and physical stresses created when you deal with
criminals. A confrontation in this business may cause not only
bruised egos but also broken bones or even more serious injuries. But the financial and psychic rewards are great if you are
willing to deal with the problems.

One major consideration when forming your business is
whether to arm your security guards. Although armed guards may
be seen as a more effective deterrent to crime, they are an
additional stress factor and add to your liability insurance costs
because you and your guard are jointly responsible for whatever
the guard does with his or her weapon. Make sure you discuss
this aspect of the business with your attorney and insurance
company.

Ask potential customers for ninety-day trial agreements. Prepare an agreement that automatically goes to two years if they
are pleased with the results. Their incentive for entering into a

two-year agreement is that you will hold your hourly rate constant
for the two-year period (except for a modest cost-of-living increase).

Because you have two-year contracts in place, your security
guard company will have a great deal of value should you decide
to sell your business. I recommend that you form a corporation,
since the potential liability can be significant. False arrests,
physical-injury lawsuits, and workers' compensation claims are
commonplace in this business. Make certain that you comply
with state law and buy workers' compensation insurance.

For your payroll requirements, talk to your local bank about
their payroll program. Many banks will calculate employee withholding, print the employee checks, and mail them to you on a
weekly or biweekly basis. The bank simply debits your account
for the gross amount. Some banks debit at the time they print
the check, while others debit your account as the checks are
cashed. Needless to say, you want the payroll program that debits
as checks are cashed, so you can keep your money longer.

RESOURCES

International Association for Hospital Security
P.O. Box 637
Lombard, IL 60148
(708) 953-0990

Security
Cahners Publishing
44 Cook St.
Denver, CO 80206-5800
(303) 388-4511

SECURITY GUARD BUSINESS LAUNCH CHECKLIST

☐ See attorney to form corporation.
☐ Open a checking account.
☐ Obtain an IRS tax identification number from your local IRS
office.

☐ Order business cards and stationery.

☐ Discuss with your attorney the terms of your two-year customer contract.

☐ Pick up fingerprint cards from your local police station for your new employees to fill out and submit to your state compliance office.

☐ Contact insurance agency about bond requirements.

☐ Contact insurance agency about workers' compensation insurance and general liability insurance.

☐ Contact city and state for licensure requirements.

☐ Arrange with artist to lay out brochure.

☐ Contact uniform company to arrange for discounts and favorable financing terms for purchases.

☐ Contact state unemployment office for prospective employees.

☐ Write a business plan. Incorporate the knowledge gained from work accomplished on your checklist.

12

Private Detective Agency

Have you ever wondered what it would be like to be a private detective? How would it feel to uncover a clue that helps locate a missing person, frees a falsely accused suspect, or puts a criminal behind bars? In America today there is a tremendous need for "private eyes," a term inspired in the 1850s by the trademark of the legendary Allan Pinkerton agency: "The Eye That Never Sleeps." Why the great demand?

- City police departments are so overloaded with cases that justice cannot always be served. According to the California Association of Licensed Investigators in Sacramento, California, private detectives help solve a great percentage of the criminal cases in the United States.
- White-collar crime is a growing concern for American industry. In the United States, according to the ABC "Nightly News," employees are responsible for seven times more theft in retail stores than nonemployees. Every day employees are found embezzling, stealing trade secrets, sabotaging projects. According to top federal regulators, fraud caused as much as 60 percent of all savings and loan failures in 1989. By assembling financial profiles of S&L executives, private investigators can recover large sums of money by sifting through paper trails where overworked prosecutors must leave off.
- Insurance fraud costs the American public an estimated $15 billion each year. Recently Pinkerton's announced plans to expand its private investigation unit into insurance investigation because of the high profit margins.
- There is a growing need for and corresponding availability of information about individual citizens. The advent of database services coupled with the affordability of personal computers

has made such information more accessible to private investigators. For example, Investigators On-Line Network (ION) is a worldwide information exchange for private investigators searching for specific data such as the location of individuals running to avoid child-care payments, spouses hiding assets from one another, or adopted children seeking their natural parents.

- The federal government's internal investigative branches are chronically understaffed. The nature of the modern political campaign dictates that one candidate know all there is to know about the personal and professional lives of his or her opponents. As a result, private eyes are making increasingly frequent appearances in the political affairs arena. Parvus Company, founded in 1984 by Gerard P. Burke, specializes in international intelligence work for U.S. corporations, producing reports that outline the political and economic climate in a foreign country at a cost to the client of $5,000 to $36,000. Opportunities in private investigation are global, vast, diversified, and exciting. With multinational, United States–based corporations building plants and investing money in foreign countries, the need for firms like Parvus is outstripping the supply of good investigators.

For those who can meet the demand for factual information through research and investigation, the financial rewards can be quite handsome.

Increasingly, private detectives are using on-line databases to help solve cases. For example, Intertect, a Texas-based private investigation agency, has access to approximately four hundred database services such as Information America, Dialog, Accu-Search, Vutext, and Standard and Poor's. For a nominal fee, companies like Information Resource Service Company (IRSC) in Fullerton, California (telephone [714] 526-8485) can perform credit checks and criminal background checks. They can tell you when someone was born, everything on the person's motor vehicle report, and when he or she died. All of this may be retrieved with one simple call if you are a licensed private detective. Databases enable private detectives to process large volumes of information, which increases their revenues.

Most states require that you meet certain licensing requirements to become a private detective. They usually require a set
of fingerprints and conduct a computer search to verify that you
have no criminal history. Depending upon how much money you
want to spend and how much time you have, in most major U.S.
cities you can enroll in private-detective schools with courses
lasting from two months to two years. Many states also require
that you have investigative experience in police work or in a
state or federal agency for a minimum amount of time. In California, for example, you have to demonstrate six thousand hours of
on-the-job experience. Many detective agencies will hire ap-
prentices, so you can train under a licensed detective.

Your initial assignments will probably be limited to fact-finding
research and surveillance. Don't despair: in most agencies you
will quickly graduate to more exciting work as you successfully
demonstrate your abilities. In addition to working as an apprentice, you can find a number of great books on how to investigate
everything from arson to murder.

When I started Whitlock Investigations, I had no experience as
an investigator, but I had been operating a security guard business and had been a police officer. My related experience qualified me to take the private investigators' state examination.
According to the Bureau of Collections and Investigative Services
in Sacramento, California, the failure rate for the state exam is
about 50 percent.

I called Dan Merit, a local supersleuth whom I had found in the
yellow pages, and asked him if he would tutor me. Dan specialized in locating missing children, a lucrative business judging by
his plush offices and custom-made suits. For $250, he gave me
four hours of his time, and I passed the examination with only
two wrong answers. How was I supposed to know which side of
an automobile block the serial number is on or what legal rights
a private citizen has when making a citizen's arrest?

Because I owned a security guard business specializing in
hospital security, I decided to specialize in malpractice and
hospital investigations, without a doubt one of the most interesting businesses I ever owned. I promoted security guards who
demonstrated good work habits and competent behavioral pat-

terns to the position of detective. We apprehended surgeons stealing operating instruments for their off-premises abortion clinics, caught nurses selling drugs inside and outside of the hospital, and we caught one chef red-handed as he was loading two cases of steaks into the trunk of his car. One pathology laboratory was preprinting test results; the staff would take a patient's money but never ran any of the prescribed tests.

Once you have some experience under your belt, you might consider specializing. Some private detectives concentrate on finding the natural parents of adopted children, while others specialize in skip tracing, which is locating missing people. Credit investigations is another lucrative field to consider. Insurance investigations and telephone and computer security are other possibilities.

Once you receive your state license, you should contact attorneys who specialize in your area of interest. For example, if you want to specialize in personal injury, you would contact lawyers whose specialty is personal injury, or phone divorce attorneys if you want to concentrate in the area of divorce investigations. Many yellow pages directories separate attorneys by their specialty. Others carry display ads that state the areas of expertise of each firm.

Most private detectives advertise in the yellow pages and report good results. If you want to specialize in just one area of investigation, you may elect to lay out a simple one-page brochure for distribution to potential customers in that investigative category. If you elect to work in a number of areas, you should design a more elaborate brochure.

Before you start a private detective agency, you should acquire some experience. Work either as an apprentice for a private detective agency, with an insurance company as a claims investigator, or in a department store in inventory control or security. Insurance companies frequently hire private detectives to determine whether or not a workers' compensation claim is legitimate. If someone claims he injured his back on the job and can't work anymore and you take a photograph of the claimant lifting garbage cans or changing tires, he may not receive full benefits—or any benefits for that matter. Insurance companies also hire private detectives to investigate reported thefts, since it is not uncommon for someone to fake a theft to collect on an insurance policy. One desperate man in England actually chopped off the lower half of his leg in order to collect on his insurance policy. He claimed that something fell out of a window and cut his leg off. Even though a jury found him guilty of fraud, they let him go because they felt that his punishment was severe enough under the circumstances.

Initially, you can work out of your home and use a post office box for handling correspondence. You can arrange to meet clients at their offices or in restaurants. You may inquire about sharing offices with a security guard company in your area. In addition to lower rent, you can share secretarial and phone-answering expenses. As your business grows and you begin to prosper, you can rent your own office.

Check with your state's bureau of licensing to find out whether you must obtain a general liability insurance policy to protect you from lawsuits. Bonding also may be required. Depending upon the type of investigations you enter, you may need additional insurance, so check with a reputable insurance firm.

Many private detectives make six-figure incomes. Annual revenues at Parvus Company exceed $1 million. The company employs ten full-time professionals, and its largest job was a $500,000 investigation of a shipping company that was scuttling its own ships to collect insurance monies. Typically, private detectives charge between $95 and $265 per hour. Some criminal specialists charge as much as $500 per hour. Detectives usually charge their industrial, legal, and insurance clients monthly retainers, then allocate a block of hours each month to each client. One detective in New York charges bail bondsmen 20 percent of the bond and all expenses when locating and apprehending criminals who have skipped bond. As you might expect, he is one of the detectives who enjoys a six-figure income.

RESOURCES

International Security and Detective Alliance
P.O. Box 6303
Corpus Christi, TX 78466
(512) 888-6164

National Association of Investigative Specialists
P.O. Box 33244
Austin, TX 78764
(512) 832-0355

National Council of Investigation and Security Services
P.O. Box 449
Severna Park, MD 21146
(800) 445-8408

World Association of Detectives
P.O. Box 1049
Severna Park, MD 21146
(800) 962-0516

Police & Security News
1690 Quarry Rd.
P.O. Box 330
Kulpsville, PA 19443
(215) 538-1240

PRIVATE DETECTIVE AGENCY LAUNCH CHECKLIST

☐ Meet with your attorney to form a corporation.
☐ Open a checking account.
☐ Visit IRS office to obtain an IRS tax identification number.
☐ Order business cards and stationery.
☐ Check with local private detective school for class information.
☐ Check with local private-detective agency, insurance company, and/or department store about an apprenticeship.
☐ Investigate licensure requirements in your state.
☐ Check with city about a business license.
☐ Check with your insurance agent about general liability insurance and costs to obtain a bond.
☐ Talk to a local security guard company about sharing their office space.
☐ Place an advertisement in the yellow pages.
☐ Check with industry associations and join local private-investigator association.
☐ Write a business plan. Incorporate the knowledge gained from work accomplished on your checklist.

13

Consulting

Why do consultants typically earn more per hour than hourly employees doing essentially the same work? Employers do not have to pay for a consultant's sick leave, holidays, and vacation time, nor do they withhold Social Security, federal and state income taxes, and disability insurance payments. Moreover, an employer doesn't have to worry about paying a consultant during slow periods or the severance pay for an employee who had to be terminated. Plus, the consultant probably won't require training, other than for orientation. The true bottom-line cost of a consultant may be less, even though the employer pays the consultant twice the rate for an employee doing the same task.

Consulting is a growing industry. During the 1980s, reports *Working Woman* (October 1989), consulting grew 16 percent annually to become an over $8 billion industry.

Whether employer or employee, each of us is looking for faster and less expensive ways to achieve our objectives. Consulting is one way of doing this. It offers the employer an efficient, benefits-free method of obtaining expertise as needed while providing the consultant with a sense of independence and generally higher wages than he or she would be receiving as a regular, full-time employee.

Almost every one of us has the ability to become a consultant. If, for example, you are a chef in a restaurant and you know how to run an efficient kitchen, buy food at the best prices, hire and train kitchen help, prepare delicious, nutritious, and unusually pleasing food, you can become a part-time (and, later, full-time) consultant. Since the number of businesses with which you are consulting may vary at any given time, you might also want to consider writing recipes, a newsletter, or magazine articles to increase your visibility while earning extra money during the slow periods.

As a chef interested in consulting, you'd approach restaurants in your community that do not represent a threat to your restaurant because of their proximity or similar cuisine. If you earn $20 per hour at your regular job, you may want to consider charging at least $40 to $50 per hour for your consulting time. Of course, this opportunity presupposes that you do not have an employment contract prohibiting you from working as a consultant in the same business. I'm also assuming you know how to prepare your client's cuisine!

I know a hairstylist who earns more money instructing new styling salon owners how to set up an efficient, well-located, properly staffed hair salon than he earns running his own salon. For him, the big payoff is the great feeling of independence. The downside risk, of course, is failing to secure cash-paying jobs.

Redirecting our existing talents is all that it takes sometimes. I know a gold prospector who could find gold nuggets with his gold pan after professional mining companies dredged the rock bottoms of riverbeds for months. He set up a gold-panning booth at a local county fair. He put $20 worth of gold dust in his eight-foot-long trough and taught folks how to pan for gold at $2 per try. He made over $6,000 in three weeks, and when the county fair closed and the concessionaires moved to the next county, he moved with them. Today, Tom Tilden owns over fifty gold-panning troughs and runs his concessions year-round all over the United States and Canada. Last year he grossed over $3 million. Old prospector Tom had never made over $15,000 per year in his life prospecting, in spite of his gold-panning talents. Today he earns one hundred times that in profits annually. (See Chapter 27, "Gold Panning.")

During one of my recent seminars in Chicago, I was asked by a real estate salesperson what she could do as a consultant. Sarah had been selling real estate for less than six months. She was a computer-training specialist and had been fired for excessive absenteeism caused by her caring for her terminally ill son. I suggested that she combine her computer skills and her real estate skills and start a computerized home buyers' program.

The program would save real estate agents time by enabling them to close sales earlier while helping the buyer to narrow down the search for the right home in the comfort of the agent's office. The more I thought about it, the more excited everyone in the class (myself included) became.

Here's how it would work. A photographer would take pictures of all new listings (which normally was done anyway). Sarah would input all the listing information, such as price, square footage, description of the home, what was included in the price, financing terms, distance to schools, churches, synagogues, transportation, shopping centers, tax structure, and so on.

The buyer would come in and view the photos. After selecting one or two homes that looked good, the buyer would discuss his or her specific needs with the real estate agent, who would input the needs into the computer and match them up with the sellers' specifications. Once a computer match was made, the real estate agent would show the homes. If the buyer wanted to make an offer, he or she would return to the agent's office and sign an offer. The seller was called, and if the seller agreed, the agent could access a credit report by calling one of the many credit-reporting agencies, ask the computer to search the current financing programs available, and offer the buyer the best terms available to him or her at that time.

Sarah added one small feature to the concept. She actually obtained a computerized loan approval before the prospective buyer left her office. Sarah turned this idea into a great business and now makes more money in a month than she used to make in a year.

The key is to match your talents with a marketing need. Just think about what this real estate agent did for everyone involved in this transaction:

- The buyer spent considerably less time looking at homes.
- The seller had a prequalified buyer and didn't have to take the property off the market while waiting for credit approval.
- The seller had an answer the same day the offer was made.
- The lending entity was able to write more mortgage contracts.
- The real estate agent sold more property faster.
- Shorter escrows resulted, due to preapproval of financing.

Perhaps you, too, can match your existing skills with a marketing opportunity and, like Sarah, find financial security. Sarah is now developing a special software package that will eventually be sold to real estate agents all over the United States, with a small 10 to 20 percent markup for herself. Sarah won't have to worry about being fired when a personal tragedy strikes or, for that matter, about selling real estate.

Are there some computer applications that would make your tasks more effective, easier, faster, more profitable? If so, your peers may be willing to pay you for developing them.

I know of no hard and fast guidelines to determine how much to bill for your services. Since you're probably delivering intangible goods, you may wish to base your fees on an hourly or daily rate. Common alternatives to this are fixed-price contracts, performance contracts, and cost-plus-percentage contracts. Whatever method is used, make sure that you pay yourself for your labor, which has a specific value whether you're working for yourself or someone else. To arrive at a daily rate of pay, determine what your annual salary would be if you were working for someone else, and divide that by the number of paid days per year (usually 261). Then figure in your overhead costs, which typically run anywhere from 65 to 145 percent of your daily rate. It may also help if you establish a standard fee schedule for specific routine tasks. Last but not least: Don't forget to add in your profit, which could be a 10 to 25 percent margin.

If you have no competition in your field of expertise, you may well be able to charge whatever the market will bear; if you are offering consulting services in a highly competitive market, you will need to establish more competitive fees. Do some research to find out what the current accepted rates are in your industry in your city. The organizations listed at the end of this chapter offer assistance to consultants on how to set fees, get referrals, and so forth. Once you develop a good track record, you'll be able to justify higher fees than you can initially.

Depending upon what line of consulting you enter, you may wish to contact an attorney about the need for formal contracts with your clients to spell out exactly what the client expects, what you are to deliver when, and the terms of payment. Keep detailed notes of all conversations with your clients (especially those concerning billings), and follow up what you consider important conversations with written confirmation.

Turn your most marketable skill into a profitable consulting business. You, like Tom Tilden, might find a gold mine!

RESOURCES

American Association of Professional Consultants
9140 Ward Pkwy.
Kansas City, MO 64114
(913) 648-2679

American Consultants League
1290 Palm Ave.
Sarasota, FL 34236
(813) 952-9290

Institute of Management Consultants
230 Park Ave. #544
New York, NY 10169
(212) 697-8262

Survey of Current Business
U.S. Government Printing Office
Superintendent of Documents
Washington, DC 20402
(202) 783-3238

CONSULTING BUSINESS LAUNCH CHECKLIST

☐ Form a sole proprietorship.
☐ Open a bank account.
☐ Contact the IRS to obtain your tax identification number.
☐ Meet with printer to design a brochure. Order business cards and stationery.
☐ Meet with your attorney to have a consulting agreement drafted.
☐ Contact your city business office to determine whether a license is required.

☐ File a DBA with a local newspaper.
☐ Analyze competitive consulting businesses if they exist in your community.
☐ Contact potential clients to determine their level of interest.
☐ Contact the industry associations for help and guidance.
☐ Write a business plan. Incorporate the knowledge gained from work accomplished on your checklist.

14
Magazine Publishing

With the advent of desktop publishing software programs, starting a magazine is easier than ever before. Of course, the downside is that it's easy for others to get into this business as well, and that means competition. The Magazine Publishers Association reports that in 1989 alone there were over one hundred new consumer magazines introduced in the United States.

In the past in order for a magazine to be laid out, typed articles had to be typeset. An art director designed the pages, photographers shot their assignments, artists created the drawings, a traffic coordinator determined the placement of advertisements using an office or hallway wall, graphics personnel pasted up the typeset copy, positioning the art and photographs on the pages. Then a magazine was ready for the printer. Today with the use of a Macintosh or IBM computer, pages are designed on a computer screen rather than through the traditional methods of typesetting, pasteup, and page creation. These computers can reproduce near-typeset-quality printouts of what's been envisioned. You can get programs that can analyze the advertising traffic needs and select specific locations for ads within the magazine. Basically, the computer can be used to get a magazine from concept to camera-ready art. All of this can be accomplished *at home on your computer*. Now you know why there are over 2,200 magazines in the U.S. market today!

Unless you know exactly what computer equipment you want, you'll probably want to rent or lease equipment and test various programs before you decide to buy, because it will be an investment. The *Folio Source Book* (published by *Folio* magazine—call [203] 358-9900) is a guide to products, services, and equipment in the magazine publishing industry and could be of tremendous help to you in launching your project. Subscribe to at least one of the magazines targeted specifically to desktop publishers; you'll find a list of a few of these at the end of this chapter. Contact other publishers who are designing their magazines using desktop programs, and query their art directors and production managers about how the equipment is operating for them, what applications they're using, what they like and don't like, and any other specific questions that might help you decide what equipment you should select for your magazine.

Your magazine will fit into one of the two basic categories of magazines: consumer or trade. Consumer magazines are sold on newsstands and are designed for the general public. *Entrepreneur* magazine, for example, is purchased by men and women who are either already in business for themselves or who would like to go into business for themselves. Trade magazines, on the other hand, are aimed at vertical industrial or professional markets. A magazine for dentists and other dental professionals is an illustration of a trade magazine.

Advertisers will often pay more per thousand readers for an advertisement in a trade magazine than they will pay in a consumer magazine. The reason is that a trade magazine goes to a highly targeted audience. If you sold psychology tests, you would probably choose to advertise in a psychology trade magazine rather than in a more general, consumer magazine. On the other hand, if you are an automobile manufacturer, you would certainly advertise in consumer publications. With the number of magazines on the market today, is it any wonder that advertisers hire advertising agencies to place their ads for them? The agency typically charges the customer for all creative work (artwork, layout, and ad concept design) and charges the magazine a 15 percent commission for placing the advertisement with them. The advertising agency has full-time media buyers who analyze the magazines on the market and decide which ones get what portion of each client's advertising budget.

In most major cities throughout the United States, there are independent publisher's representatives who will sell advertising space for you on a straight commission basis. Normally, the magazine publisher pays the independent representative a 20 percent commission thirty days after receiving payment from the advertiser. So, if you use independent representatives, your sales expense will consist of 20 percent to the representative and 15 percent to the ad agency. That gives you a net of 65 percent of the advertising rate that you charge your advertisers.

The circulation of many trade magazines is controlled, meaning that the only source of earnings comes from advertising revenue. Another option is to sell a magazine without any advertising to paid subscribers and perhaps newsstand buyers. Thus, your earning will come solely from subscription and newsstand revenue. Your third and final choice is to publish a magazine that sells space for advertising and charges for copies sold. Both of my past magazine publishing projects, *HeartCorps* and *Medical Technicians/Technologists*, fit the third category. Sometimes a new magazine will start out as a controlled circulation magazine but will convert to allow paid circulation as the demand for the product increases.

Although magazine publishing is a relatively easy business to get into, it has its downside risks. It's very competitive, and it's usually difficult to get subscribers to pay for their subscriptions. Even though cash flow problems often result due to the high cost of doing business and the fact that subscribers or advertisers have not yet paid you, you still must get your magazine out regularly.

There are many great printers in the United States that specialize in magazine printing; several are listed at the end of this chapter. Your printer should have the ability to print, bind, polybag (if required), address, insert blow-in and bind-in cards, and mail your finished product. Until your printer gets to know you and you have more experience under your belt, the printer usually will not extend credit. Standard terms for a new magazine are 50 percent with order and the balance due upon delivery.

Next, you will need to locate a fulfillment house to handle your subscription fulfillment requirements. Subscribers' names and addresses are mailed directly to these firms, which also have toll-free numbers to receive orders for new subscriptions or answer subscriber questions. Your fulfillment house will provide a list of your subscribers to your printer, who will mail out your

magazine. Three well-known fulfillment houses offering comprehensive services to a host of magazines are:

>Kable Publishers Aide
>Kable Square
>Mt. Morris, IL 61054
>(815) 734-4151

>Neodata
>833 W. South Boulder
>Louisville, CO 80027
>(303) 666-7000

>Communications Data Service
>112 10th St.
>Des Moines, IA 50309
>(515) 246-6920

To launch a magazine properly, you will need an editor, art
director, publisher, and possibly a circulation manager, if you're
selling subscriptions. You can wear all of these hats initially or
hire freelancers or employees (part-time or full-time). You can
contract with talented independent writers, who usually charge
between fifty cents and a dollar per word to write your articles.
Your editor, who makes the writing assignments and sets com-
pletion dates, probably knows writers who can write articles for
your magazine. If the editor doesn't, contact one of the authors'
associations in your area to provide you with a list of freelance
writers. The names of a couple of these associations are listed at
the end of this chapter.

Because readers may act upon what they read, there is always
some liability in publishing. Magazines may be sued for slander
and defamation of character. While the courts seldom find in
favor of the plaintiffs in these cases, the cost for defense can be
astronomical. Consider forming a corporation as a first line of
defense, and inquire about a general liability insurance policy.
The policy for *HeartCorps* magazine had an annual premium of
less than $1,200 for the essential coverage. Contracts will be
necessary with your printer, fulfillment house, independent publisher's representatives, advertisers, photographers, artists, free-

lance writers, and your distributor (if and when you decide to put your magazine on the newsstands), so contact an attorney well versed in publishing law.

You may wish to hire a publishing expert as consultant to help launch your publication. The Magazine Publishers Association in New York can help you locate a magazine consultant and also sponsors publishing seminars throughout the year. Before launching *HeartCorps*, I attended Stanford University's two-week publishing course in Palo Alto, California (call [415] 723-2300), a course that's offered only once each year. People in the industry come from all over the world to attend the classes, taught by individuals who are well known in the publishing community. You must apply for entry into the course and be selected to attend, so early registration is suggested. This course costs approximately $2,200 and is worth every cent.

The magazine industry has been threatened by the advent of new technology and media competition, yet it is still one of the most inexpensive and most popular forms of entertainment and information. Magazine publishing can be very exciting and profitable, but beware: for every success story, there are hundreds of magazines that don't make it. Eighty percent of new magazines fail before they reach the age of four. This is not a business for the fainthearted. You may want to ease into this by starting first with a newsletter or creating advertising brochures.

Before you start your business, talk to some advertising agencies about your project, and determine their level of interest in placing ads. Talk to a few independent representatives who sell advertising space, and determine their level of interest in handling your magazine. Send a mailing to a few thousand prospective subscribers, and offer them a two-year founders' subscription for the price of one year; see firsthand what kind of response you get. If these initial tests look good, and if competitive magazines are not meeting the needs of consumers, become a publisher.

Take your findings, prepare a business plan with financial pro formas, and raise some operating capital. Do not underestimate your capitalization requirements. What could be more heartbreaking than creating a beautiful magazine and then not having enough money to pay the printer? (That's one reason why I chose a *printer* as my partner for *HeartCorps* magazine!)

RESOURCES

American Society of Journalists and Authors
1501 Broadway, Ste. 302
New York, NY 10036
(212) 997-0947

Authors Guild
330 W. 42nd St.
New York, NY 10036
(212) 563-5904

Magazine Publishers Association
575 Lexington Ave.
New York, NY 10022
(212) 752-0055

National Association of Desktop Publishers
1260 Boylston St.
Boston, MA 02215
(617) 426-2885

National Association of Publishers' Representatives
200 E. 15th St., Ste. A
New York, NY 10003
(212) 505-9521

Printing Industry of America
100 Dangerfield Rd.
Alexandria, VA 22314
(703) 519-8100

Desktop Publisher
Yellowstone Information Services
7 View Dr.
Elkview, WV 25071
(304) 965-5548

Folio Magazine
Hanson Publishing Group, Inc.
6 River Bend Ctr.
Box 4949
911 Hope St.
Stamford, CT 06907-0949
(203) 358-9900

MacWorld
501 Second St.
San Francisco, CA 94107
(415) 243-0505

Magazine Week
Lighthouse Communications, Inc.
233 W. Central St.
Natick, MA 01760
(508) 650-1001

PC *World*
501 Second St.
San Francisco, CA 94107
(415) 243-0500

Publish
Integrated Media, Inc.
501 Second St.
San Francisco, CA 94107
(415) 243-0600

Publishing News
Hanson Publishing Group, Inc.
6 River Bend Ctr.
Box 4949
911 Hope St.
Stamford, CT 06907-0949
(203) 358-9900

Printers

R. R. Donnelley & Sons Co.
350 E. 22nd St.
Chicago, IL 60616
(312) 326-8000

World Color Press, Inc.
401 Industrial Dr.
P.O. Box 1248
Effingham, IL 62401
(217) 342-9241

Arcata Graphics Co.
201 N. Charles St.
Baltimore, MD 21201
(301) 783-5200

Quad/Graphics, Inc.
West 224 N. 3322 Duplainville Rd.
Pewaukee, WI 53072
(414) 691-9200

MAGAZINE PUBLISHING BUSINESS
LAUNCH CHECKLIST

- ☐ Form a corporation.
- ☐ Open a bank account.
- ☐ Purchase business cards and stationery, and prepare media kit, including advertising rate card.
- ☐ Obtain IRS tax identification number from local IRS office.
- ☐ Lease or purchase personal computer and software package if you do not already own hardware and software.
- ☐ Obtain city business license if required.
- ☐ Conduct subscriber and advertiser tests.
- ☐ Interview suppliers, including illustrators, freelance writers, photographers, mailing list brokers.
- ☐ Contact premier-issue advertisers.

☐ Contact independent publisher's representatives in New York and other major cities, and negotiate representation agreements.

☐ Join the Magazine Publishers Association and subscribe to a publication for desktop publishers.

☐ Contact printers and negotiate printing contract, including color separation, printing, binding, and delivery.

☐ Give writing assignments to freelance writers.

☐ Raise capital by selling stock, and negotiate with printer to take stock in lieu of payment for printing.

☐ Set up office in home or local office building.

☐ Contact insurance agent to buy business insurance.

☐ Write a business plan. Incorporate the knowledge gained from work accomplished on your checklist.

15

Burglar Alarm Installation and Sales

Nothing is quite as traumatic as being the victim of a crime. The National Crime Prevention Council predicts that in a twenty-year period, seven out of ten households will be burglarized at least once. Although there are professional burglars who are able to enter any home, given enough time, no matter what a homeowner does, thanks to autodial systems that are remotely activated, amateur and career criminals alike have good reason to consider an alternative profession. Today, systems can electronically detect an unauthorized entry and automatically dial the central station of the alarm service, which summons the police. This enables the police to arrest the criminal even before he or she leaves your home with all your worldly possessions.

State-of-the-art electronics coupled with our society's inability to cope with rising crime have caused the security industry to flourish. For your protection against personal attacks, not only is there Mace, but also stun guns and hand-held siren blasters that could summon Scotland Yard from a New York subway.

Businesses, too, have jumped on the high-tech security system bandwagon. Familiar to us all are the continuous-coverage closed-circuit television cameras that banks use to record every customer's transaction, including those all-too-frequent unauthorized withdrawals. Frank Jones, considered a guru of electronic surveillance and owner of The Spy Shop in Manhattan, has adapted a Sony camcorder with a Video Scope attachment that enables surveillance in total darkness from five blocks away— even through window shades. More hotels than ever are using card access to their rooms instead of numbered keys that can be misplaced; if a card key is lost, it is simply voided in the master controller. Many hotels are also installing safes in individual rooms for convenience and safety.

Residential security is the fastest growing segment of the young security industry. According to STAT Resources, a Brookline, Massachusetts, firm, residential security provided about $2.5 billion of 1989's $8.4 billion industry revenues. The $250 Electronic Watchdog uses a microchip with a German shepherd's bark to discourage unauthorized entry into the home. The small box is placed by the door. If anyone approaches, it will start barking. The closer the approach, the more ferocious the barking becomes. A homeowner can tape his windows so that when any of them is opened, the alarm goes off. Wireless motion-detector kits, which are available from Intelectron of Hayward, California, allow homeowners to add security to areas such as the backyard where wiring is difficult. Switches can be placed under carpets so that when an intruder steps on one, the alarm goes off. Doors, walls, and ceilings can be wired so that illegal entry cannot be made without an alarm going off. The alarm can be as simple as a bell clanging or as sophisticated as the police being silently summoned by an autodialer system.

Well over four million vehicles are stolen or have their contents or accessories stolen every year, according to FBI statistics. Depending upon the sophistication of its features, a car security system will range in price from about $100 to $1,000. Teletrac (call [800] 800-7500) recently introduced a new burglar-tracking system for automobiles. When an unauthorized entry is made into your vehicle, a device mounted on the car sends a signal telling the central station operator the precise location of your car. Just imagine a thief stealing your car from a restaurant parking lot shortly after you have arrived for a dinner engagement. The central station operator calls the police and tells them that your vehicle is going south on Main Street. The police follow the operator's directions as your car turns up and down streets. The police stop the car, arrest the driver, and ask the central station operator where the car was stolen from. Before your dessert arrives, your car is returned to the parking lot.

The burglar alarm industry is growing at an all-time rate. It's a great business even during recessionary times, because as unemployment rises, there is a corresponding increase in crime. As times get tougher for other people, they get better for the burglar alarm companies. And, thanks to new modular systems and sensors, in recent years household systems have become more readily available and cheaper.

Once you decide what type of legal entity to use for your new business, you will be ready to select the equipment you want to sell. Your attorney will assist you in deciding whether to form a corporation, sole proprietorship, or partnership. Because of the potential liability, it's likely that he or she will recommend that you form a corporation to minimize your personal liability.

Assuming you have had no experience with burglar alarms and security equipment, I suggest that you attend one of the many national security conventions and business expositions. Dates and locations can usually be obtained from one of three well-known security magazines: *Security*, *Security Distributing & Marketing* (both published by Cahners in Denver, CO; [303] 388-4511), and *Security Sales* (Bobit Publishing Company, Redondo Beach, CA; [213] 376-8788). These conventions are not usually open to the general public, so you will need to have business cards printed before attending. Go from booth to booth, comparing wholesale prices, service capabilities, catalogs, literature, and bells and whistles. You may be able to actually negotiate distributorships at the show. On my first visit to a security convention in Los Angeles, I negotiated the distributorship for over thirty lines of security products at 25 to 50 percent discounts.

You should be able to find a number of security consultants in the yellow pages under "Security Systems." For a fee starting as low as $25 per hour, a consultant will assist you in selecting the best equipment to get you started in the burglar alarm business.

This industry offers people with all types of personalities, training, and ambition a specialty area just for them. For example, if you want to repair and install burglar alarms, you should be prepared to attend a technical college and learn the fundamental electronics required by the manufacturers to repair their equipment. If you simply want to offer a security consulting service and subcontract all repairs, installation, and systems design work, that is a lucrative business all by itself. Some people specialize in installing closed-circuit television systems for banks; a two-week in-factory training program may qualify you for that business.

If you have an expressive or driver type of personality and your talents run toward sales, you may want to become an independent representative for security services and products. You could work out an arrangement to sell basic home burglar alarms for a distributor for half of the company's factory discount. Make similar arrangements with distributors of card access equipment, closed-circuit televisions, safes, auto alarms, and even security guard services, then act as a security program broker. Most of these distributors would be anxious to provide training.

There are several manufacturers of card access security systems that are generally used only for business and industry. Cardkey (101 W. Cochran Rd., Simi Valley, CA 93065; [805] 522-5555) is the oldest card access company in the United States. The company offers systems that allow basic entry by sliding a card similar to a credit card through a slot, causing a door to open. They have a full range of access equipment for businesses, including one that not only gives the cardholder access but records who the person is, the date and time of access, and the time the person leaves the premises. UPS and Federal Express even monitor their drivers' access to fuel pumps by card access. Tremendous opportunities exist in this industry.

Once you have selected your product lines, you need to market and sell your products and/or installation services. Many manufacturers offer training programs on installing and servicing their equipment. Servicing usually consists of troubleshooting with a symptoms guide. Frequently, replacing a defective printed circuit board will correct the problem. You send the malfunctioning board back to the manufacturer, which replaces it with a working board so that you are prepared for the next service call.

While my next suggestion may smack of ambulance chasing, it is very effective; if handled with a certain amount of diplomacy and tact, it will not be offensive to your potential customers. All local papers report some percentage of the crime that occurs in the community. Police records are public and therefore, in most communities, available for public review. Get the names of recent victims of burglary, muggings, and rape, and call on them. Their greatest fear is usually that the criminal will come back, so they will welcome the kinds of precautions and protection you offer.

Contact the alarm response companies and offer your services. These companies make their money by monitoring their customers' alarms twenty-four hours a day, seven days a week for a monthly fee, usually $20 to $35 per month. Their sales force is calling on hundreds of potential burglar alarm customers every year. Many of these firms do their own installation, while others subcontract sales and installation of equipment to other companies. The burglar alarm installer usually pays them a 10 to 20 percent finder's fee for referrals.

One company in Detroit gives lectures on the best ways to secure homes and businesses, recounting true crime stories to senior citizens' clubs, Rotary and Optimist Clubs, Jaycees, and fraternal organizations. I remember attending one lecture where the alarm company's vice president of sales discussed the burglary of an insurance agency's computer hardware and software. It took the agent over a year to reinput the information—at a cost *five times* greater than the value of the hardware. One of the attendees was an insurance agent who immediately recognized how traumatic a similar theft would be for his firm. At the end of the lecture, he cornered the vice president and purchased a $12,000 burglar alarm system and agreed to initiate a program for duplicating his disks and keeping them in a safe place.

Many manufacturers will help defray your advertising expenses by paying one-half of the actual cost to purchase an advertisement in your local paper or a regional magazine. You may want to make sales calls on security guard service companies, since they are in contact with owners and managers of factories, hospitals, stores, and construction companies. Network with each company's principals, since they are often asked for sources of electronic security equipment, and offer them a 10 to 20 percent referral commission.

You may want to give some brochures to the local cardiologists' offices and hospitals in your area to be distributed to people who may live alone and have medical problems. Perhaps they need the security of owning an emergency communications system. In this business, you need to network with police, physicians, and principals of alarm response companies and security guard companies.

Depending on where you are located, installation rates vary between $40 and $90 per hour per installer, with the average rate being $60. Usually installation charges are factored into the purchase price of the system, so you as the subcontractor would collect your installation fee from the contractor. However, service and installation of additional units may be billed on an hourly basis.

Hardwire installations usually require two workers. If you are going into the installation business, you will need a truck or van (which you can probably purchase used for less than $8,000). You will need typical installation tools like wire strippers, wire cutters, and pliers. You will also need several spools of wire, with the sizes varying according to the manufacturer's installation instructions. While some manufacturers do not have training programs for installers, they can usually put you in contact with an installer outside your market area. Offer your services free of charge for two or three weeks, and learn installation techniques on the job.

The average installation of a burglar alarm in a home today has become fairly affordable. Using $3,200 as the purchase price plus up to $500 installation revenue, if you install two burglar alarms per week, you will earn $384,800 per year in gross revenues. Assuming you earn a 40 percent discount on the hardware and do your own installation, you will net $1,280 per system plus $500 per installation, earning $133,120 on the hardware and an additional $52,000 on installations in one year, for a total gross of $185,120. Even after referral commissions and paying your installer assistant, you should net over $150,000.

Many states require a license to sell and install burglar alarm systems. Check with a local, reputable installer, and ask that person what licenses he or she has. If there is no installer in your community, contact the state bureau of consumer affairs in your state capital. Also investigate the need for a general liability insurance policy of $1 million to $2 million to protect you should one of your alarm systems fail to operate properly in a burglary or should other emergencies materialize.

American psychologist Abraham H. Maslow's theory of the hierarchy of needs states that before people seek to fulfill the higher needs of belonging, love, and self-actualization, they must satisfy their physiological, safety, and protection needs relatively well. In our materialistic society, many people have costly goods to protect, and the concern over personal safety is at an all-time high. The burglar alarm business can be a great business because it can offer a great deal of personal satisfaction and monetary rewards as well as meet this dramatic human need to protect what one has earned.

RESOURCES

Security Equipment Industry Association
2800 28th St., #124
Santa Monica, CA 90405
(213) 450-4141

BURGLAR ALARM INSTALLATION AND SALES
BUSINESS LAUNCH CHECKLIST

- ☐ See your attorney about forming a corporation.
- ☐ Open a checking account.
- ☐ Contact the IRS to obtain an IRS tax identification number.
- ☐ Sell stock if you desire equity financing.
- ☐ Look into purchasing a van if you do not own one.
- ☐ Contact your insurance agent about appropriate insurance to meet your specific requirements.
- ☐ Contact your city business office about licensure requirements.
- ☐ Contact the police department about burglar alarm permit requirements.
- ☐ Check with your state board of equalization about obtaining a resale tax permit so that you can collect sales tax.
- ☐ Subscribe to at least one security magazine.
- ☐ Order business cards, stationery, and brochures.
- ☐ Attend one of the security business expositions in your area, and negotiate equipment discounts and factory training where applicable.

☐ Contact a local security business consultant to help you select appropriate security equipment. Criteria for selection of equipment will be your financial resources, background, knowledge of equipment, and installation information.

☐ Contact security equipment distributors to determine their interest in working with you as a subdistributor.

☐ Contact a card access company.

☐ Contact alarm response companies to determine their interest in referring customers to you.

☐ Contact local fraternal and civic organizations about giving security lectures.

☐ Talk to your suppliers about cooperative advertising programs.

☐ Distribute brochures to cardiologists, hospitals, alarm companies, and security guard companies.

☐ Make sales calls on security guard companies.

☐ Write a business plan. Incorporate the knowledge gained from work accomplished on your checklist.

16

Business Brokerage

Businesses are sold for a variety of reasons. The Department of Commerce reports that in the United States one out of four businesses changes hands every five years. Sometimes companies are ordered sold to pay delinquent taxes or to satisfy division of property judgments in probate court or divorce court. Many times the owner simply wants to retire.

Whatever the reason, the seller wants to find a qualified buyer as soon as possible. The seller may place an ad in the local newspaper or trade papers or put a sign in the business's window. Or the seller can hire *you* as a business broker. For a negotiated percentage of the sale price (usually between 10 and 15 percent), you agree to help the seller find a qualified buyer.

I know business brokers who make hundreds of thousands of dollars every year, while top brokers make annual commissions of half a million dollars or more. It is a perfect business for salespeople who are good negotiators.

Although this is a growth business that you can enter with very little money, what it does require is a solid understanding of business principles. It is generally recommended that you work for an established business brokerage firm before starting your own business if you feel that your knowledge of business finance and law as they apply to business sales is lacking. A real estate license also is a plus, since some states may require business brokers to have such a license or equivalent training. Consider taking a course in business brokering and/or real estate at your local college or university. There are also consultants and organizations that offer training and a variety of support services; check in your yellow pages under "Business Brokers."

You should feel comfortable evaluating balance sheets, profit and loss statements, and other financial statements before you start this business. As you get started, you may want to talk to a local accountant to assist you in interpreting financial statements for a percentage of your commission, payable as you close deals.

Advertise the seller's business in the local newspapers, along with other businesses listed with you. Because you are a regular, frequent advertiser, you should receive rates much less than the sellers could get individually. As potential buyers respond to an ad, you meet with them at their homes or offices and discuss the business opportunity in detail. Many times the seller will receive an amount of cash at the time of sale (usually 25 to 40 percent of the purchase price), and the buyer will sign a note payable to the seller in monthly installments. This often helps the seller, who pays tax only on the income actually received each year and can therefore spread his or her tax liability over a period of years (see Chapter 5, "How to Buy an Existing Business Without Money"). You will also ask the potential buyer for copies of his or her personal tax returns for the past two years so that you can demonstrate to the seller that this is indeed a qualified buyer.

In matching buyers and sellers, you may want to subscribe to one or more business listing services that provide names of companies for sale all over the United States. Later on, you'll find that you'll also get many of your clients from attorney and accountant referrals. As the industry grows, it is becoming more specialized and professional. If you decide to specialize in one area—for example, medical and dental company sales—you would advertise in journals and newsletters in that target market.

Most buyers are looking for a business that will be around for a while. Not many serious buyers would buy a "Pet Rock" type of business, so you'll need to demonstrate the company's stability to the potential buyer. The buyer will look for long-term contracts and a solid customer base. For example, if J. C. Penney has been buying the company's slippers for the past ten years and has ordered next year's design, the seller has a pretty stable customer.

A buyer should also be looking for a reasonable return on investment. For example, investing $100,000 in a business that earned 4 percent profits after taxes on sales of $100,000 isn't too exciting, since a buyer could invest that same money in tax-exempt municipal bonds and earn almost twice as much without the risk and tax liability. However, if the prospective business were to earn 20 percent after tax, a buyer would get pretty excited. That return would mean that the buyer could invest $100,000 and earn $20,000 per year, giving them a return on investment (ROI) of 20 percent. After less than five years, due to compounding, the investment would be returned. If we compounded the buyer's return over the five years, he or she would earn close to 24 percent per year, or $118,752 over the five years.

With your attorney's help, prepare a listing agreement wherein the seller agrees to pay your sales commission out of escrow. Just as a real estate agent prepares a sales sheet listing all of the features and benefits of a home, your sales sheet would list all of the selling features and benefits of owning the business. The sales sheet will list the inventory, work in progress, in-house contracts, equipment, buildings, fixtures, leasehold improvements (improvements to the buildings), and other assets and liabilities. Attach resumes of the management, income tax statements, and profit and loss statements from the previous two years, a current balance sheet, and financial projections if available. The company's controller can prepare these for you. If you have to hire an accountant to do some of this work, charge a higher commission on the sale.

Take photographs of the buildings, stores, offices, and equipment. Have your independent accountant give you an honest appraisal of the company's worth. An unrealistic value will undermine your sales efforts. Often owners overvalue their companies, but it is also possible that the seller will underestimate the value. This is often seen with older, retiring owners who purchased their building when it was worth perhaps one-tenth of what it is currently worth. An independent appraisal is usually worth the cost, and you may be able to persuade the seller to pay for such an appraisal.

Not all businesses are sold in the same manner, so make sure you're familiar with the standards of the particular industry. For instance, magazines are sometimes sold for a certain dollar amount per subscriber, regardless of the company's profits and losses. Sometimes professional businesses are purchased for a multiple of earnings. A law firm may earn $200,000 per year. A typical sale may be at four times earnings, or, in this case, $800,000. I have sold businesses on a straight asset-minus-liability basis. For example, my business had $1,000,000 in assets with $400,000 in liabilities; I received a check for $600,000. I have also sold businesses for their contract value only. I had a security business with customer contracts extending out two and three years. The seller and I calculated the profit in the contracts, and he wrote me a check for an estimated percentage of the profits and took over the accounts. Ask the seller about the industry standards. If he is unfamiliar with standard practice, phone his professional association(s), and speak with his attorney and accountant.

Marketing your business brokerage is the easiest step of all. Fortunately there is little competition in most areas of the country, and entry into the business is easy. Simply contact business owners who are advertising their businesses for sale in the business opportunities section of the newspaper. Just as employment agencies advertise right alongside nonagencies, you will be advertising right alongside your potential clients. Describe your services and the benefits of using a broker. Remind potential customers that, just as they wouldn't sell their own home, they shouldn't be selling their own business either.

Send a letter of introduction to the lawyers in your community. They not only handle probate and divorce matters but also work very closely with corporations, so they are familiar with which ones are opening, closing, and relocating. Give lectures at Rotary Club or chamber of commerce luncheons: these can be very productive from a networking standpoint.

You may want to visit with a business brokerage agent outside of your market area and get some pointers from someone already in the business. Who knows? That person may want to expand into your area; perhaps the two of you could enter into a joint venture. Your partner's firm could provide the operating capital while you provide the "human capital."

This is a fun and lucrative business for an entrepreneur. It's the kind of business that you can start on a part-time basis and grow into a full-time business. Marketing costs are minimal, capital requirements are small, and the upside earning potential is substantial. One word of caution: before starting you should have enough money to cover your living expenses for at least six months, because it will probably take that long to get a business listing, sell the business, and close escrow. Fortunately, you will have listed other businesses during that six-month period, and commissions should come in on a regular basis. The checks may be slow in coming at first, but 10 percent of $1 million or $2 million is definitely worth the wait!

RESOURCES

International Business Brokers Association
P.O. Box 704
Concord, MA 01742
(508) 369-2490

Institute of Certified Business Counselors
P.O. Box 70326
Eugene, OR 97401
(503) 345-8064

BUSINESS BROKERAGE BUSINESS
LAUNCH CHECKLIST

☐ Meet with your attorney to form a corporation and have a listing agreement prepared.
☐ Open a bank account.
☐ File DBA with your local newspaper.
☐ Have business cards and stationery printed.
☐ Visit your local IRS office to obtain a tax identification number.
☐ Obtain errors and omissions insurance.
☐ Visit a local accountant if you require his or her services.
☐ Check with a local university about business and accounting courses.
☐ Call the state's real estate licensing board to determine licensure requirements.

☐ Subscribe to local newspapers. You will want to contact owners advertising their businesses for sale. Subscribe to Dun & Bradstreet or a local business paper such as *Crain's* in Chicago or New York, *Business Journal* in St. Louis, Kansas City, or San Francisco.

☐ Negotiate favorable newspaper advertising rates.

☐ Draft a form sales sheet.

☐ Check with the city licensing department to obtain a license if required.

☐ Have a simple one-page brochure laid out and printed.

☐ Send letter to accountants and lawyers advising them of your services.

☐ Contact industry associations and enlist their help.

☐ Write a business plan. Incorporate the knowledge gained from work accomplished on your checklist.

17

Water Conservation

Water is a precious commodity. Since 1980, there has been only one year—1982—where most areas of the United States received normal precipitation. Otherwise, the country has been experiencing unusually dry conditions for the past decade. By the end of 1990, California had endured a four-year drought. In some areas of California, water has been rationed and penalties imposed on customers who have not curtailed their consumption. In such an uncertain environment, it makes sense to be prepared for potential problems with your home water supply and to do everything within your power to conserve water.

What if I told you of a water-saving product that is probably already known to you in an existing, but distinctly different, application? What if I told you that the same product will cut the average homeowner's lawn-watering bill by over 50 percent while increasing the growth of grass and other plants by 19 percent and the size of flowers and vegetables by 39 percent? What if I told you that it was degradable, inert, and once implanted, it gave the user up to five years of useful life and a payback of out-of-pocket costs in nine short months?

For several years superabsorbent polymers have been used *in disposable diapers* to absorb urine. A California company is placing the same safe product in the ground; the result is a whole new industry. The company has developed a special applicator to embed the polymer below the topsoil on existing lawns, where it holds up to eight hundred times its weight in water and continuously offers water to the roots of grass, flowers, shrubbery, vegetables, and other kinds of plants. It may also be used with houseplants.

As an entrepreneur, you need to train yourself to analyze the opportunities for different applications for products familiar to you. You won't have to look far. For example, look at Post-It Notes from 3M. Although they were originally intended to be permanently glued note pads, the glue failed. As a result, a whole new market was created. Bayer aspirin may well sell as much aspirin to people who want to reduce their cardiac risks as people wishing to get rid of headaches.

Quaker Oats cereal is now sold as a cholesterol reduction food. Some bright marketing person at Bunn Coffee Maker Company sized down its restaurant model and changed the stainless steel design to plastic. The result: America's households bought the coffee makers by the truckloads. Until the late 1960s every toymaker in America made dolls solely for little girls. Then G.I. Joe took the market by storm. Suddenly it was OK for little boys to play with dolls.

Relax and let your creative juices flow. Begin to look for niche markets with existing products and services. (Also refer to Chapter 11, "Security Guard.")

Consumer Reports calculates that an average American family using municipal water can save up to $75 every year on water and sewer bills by installing low-flow shower heads and low-flush toilets. The energy savings from reduced hot water use in the shower can save up to $50 more. (**Note:** According to *Consumer Reports*, water and sewer rates vary so widely from city to city that it's not always meaningful to refer to an average dollar savings from water conservation devices.)

There are a host of companies that sell conservation devices, including shower heads with reduced flow, toilet bowl bags that reduce the amount of water required to flush the toilet, low-flow toilets, and restriction valves on water lines to washing machines and faucets. Most manufacturers will provide you with the products at 25 percent to 50 percent off the retail price. At the end of this chapter is a list of companies that manufacture water conservation and/or water-purifying products. You may wish to contact several of these for product information and distributor discount availability.

Once you have selected your product(s), contact your local water department and ask them to include a small advertisement for your water conservation devices in their routine bill mailings. Offer the department part of your discount; they will most definitely be interested in the water conservation aspect of your business, and if their charter allows, they may be very interested in securing additional revenues by helping you market your products. Call on local plumbers and give them a one-color, single-sided brochure listing your products. Give any plumber a 10 percent finder's fee if one of his or her referrals purchases your products.

Whenever you are selling your product or service—in a brochure, advertisement, telephone call, or personal sales call—remember to sell its *benefits*, not just its features. A feature is a physical characteristic, such as size, color, or appearance, while a benefit is something that promotes or enhances well-being. For example, few people buy a Mercedes or BMW because of the hardened steel frame or the 900 candlelight-powered headlights; they buy such luxury cars because of the statement the car makes about the owner's success and status. Benefits generally account for 90 percent of a customer's buying decision. (See Chapter 3, "Salesmanship.")

Put the buying opportunities in the proper perspective. In this instance, sell the *savings* benefits. For example, if a homeowner spends $500 per year on water and your water conservation devices sell for $100 and can save the homeowner 20 percent of the estimated annual water bill, the customer gets his or her money back in one year (20 percent of $500 is $100). If the estimated life of the product is five years, your customer will actually *earn* $400 in water cost savings. If water costs increase, the homeowner will obviously save more. As a point of reference, if a homeowner put that same $100 in a savings account earning 10 percent interest, at the end of the same five-year period he or she would have $161.05 compounded. Ask, "Do you want to make 10 percent on your hard-earned money or nearly 40 percent compounded?"

Also talk about the ease of installation or the fact that no special tools are necessary for installation (or whatever benefits are applicable to your specific product). And remind your customers that they are doing their part to conserve one of our most precious resources.

Don't overlook office buildings, hospitals, hotels, and public buildings as potential customers. In each case, owners and managers should be very interested in saving money on their water bills.

Another natural path may be a water purification franchise. This has been called an "industry for the nineties," because consumers are increasingly concerned about water quality. National Safety Associates, Inc. (NSA), a twenty-year-old firm based in Memphis, Tennessee (4260 E. Raines Rd., Memphis, TN 38338; [901] 366-9288), is an example of a manufacturer of home water treatment units. This company offers independent distributorships for $5,000. The initial fee includes a basic inventory of easy-to-install, inexpensive filters that attach directly to the customer's faucet. NSA also has an office water cooler that does not require the familiar five-gallon bottle. Instead, this cooler has an in-line filtration system that gives the customer comparable water without having to lift heavy water bottles. Amway (7575 E. Fulton, Ada, MI 49355; [616] 676-6000) also has a water filtration device you may wish to investigate.

Softron International (5220 Edison, Chino, CA 91710; [714] 628-0644) has two very interesting products worth considering. One is a magnet that slips over your water pipe and reduces calcium buildup in your pipes. Another product softens water without using salt, which is very corrosive as well as dangerous to individuals with certain physical ailments.

Like NSA and Amway, Softron sells its products through a multilevel marketing program. In addition to earning money on your direct product sales, you also earn money on the product sales of the people you sponsor. One of the advantages of participating in a multilevel program is that you do not have to deal with many of the administrative issues that you would have to handle if you were operating alone. For example, Softron provides customer service, product delivery, bookkeeping, sales and marketing assistance, and, most importantly, access to novel products that are not available anywhere else.

RESOURCES

Listed below are examples of other firms that manufacture water-saving products and water-purifying devices. The list is not meant to be an endorsement, nor is it exhaustive; it's merely a jumping-off point to help you get started. Visit local stores where plumbing products are sold for perhaps larger, more familiar manufacturers. Although these businesses lend themselves to operating out of your home, you may want to consider discussing a partnership with a major plumbing company in town. You may also wish to contact your state energy commission for more information about your state's water regulations.

Manufacturers of Water Conservation Products

Niagara Conservation
230 Rt. 206
Flanders, NJ 07836
(800) 831-8383

PAC/EM Shower Filter Company
931 Metro Dr.
Monterey Park, CA 91754
(818) 571-2627

Resources Conservation, Inc.
P.O. Box 71
Greenwich, CT 06836
(203) 964-0600

Whedon Products
20 Hurlbut St.
West Hartford, CT 06110
(203) 953-7606

Manufacturers of Activated Carbon Water Filters

Coast Filtration
142 Viking Ave.
Brea, CA 92621
(714) 990-4602

Cuno, Incorporated
400 Research Pkwy.
Meriden, CT 06450
(203) 237-5541

Environment Purification Systems
P.O. Box 191
Concord, CA 94522
(415) 682-7231
(800) 829-2129 (in California)

General Ecology
151 Sheree Blvd.
Lionville, PA 19341
(215) 363-7900

Nigra Enterprises
5699 Kanan Rd.
Agoura, CA 91301
(818) 889-6877

Multi-Pure
21339 Nordhoff
Chatsworth, CA 91311
(818) 341-7377

Manufacturers of Distillers

Durastill
P.O. Box 76641
Atlanta, GA 30328
(816) 454-5260

Water & Health
829 Lynnhaven Pkwy., Ste. 119
Virginia Beach, VA 23452
(800) 222-7188
(800) 523-6388 (in Virginia)

Manufacturers of Reverse Osmosis Filters

Aquathin
2800 W. Cypress Creek Rd.
Ft. Lauderdale, FL 33309
(305) 977-7997

Water Resources International, Inc.
2800 E. Chambers
Phoenix, AZ 85040
(602) 268-2580

Other Sources of Information

Environmental Protection Agency
401 M St., SW
Washington, DC 20460
(202) 382-2090

Water Quality Association
4151 Naperville Rd.
Lisle, IL 60532
(708) 505-0160

The Water Quality Association (WQA) is a trade association representing manufacturers of point-of-use water treatment devices. The WQA certifies dealers, installers, and sales representatives of water improvement systems. The WQA's Gold Seal shows that a water improvement device meets the standards set by the industry.

National Sanitation Foundation
3475 Plymouth Rd.
Ann Arbor, MI 48105
(313) 769-8010

The National Sanitation Foundation (NSF) is an independent, nonprofit testing facility that researches devices for improving water quality. The NSF mark on a product indicates that it meets industry standards.

WATER CONSERVATION BUSINESS LAUNCH CHECKLIST

☐ Form company.
☐ Open checking account.
☐ Visit IRS office to obtain tax identification number.

☐ Obtain city business license if required.

☐ Order business cards and stationery.

☐ File DBA if appropriate.

☐ Contact companies to arrange for product distributorships.

☐ Obtain resale tax permit from state board of equalization.

☐ Lay out descriptive brochure and have it printed.

☐ Contact your state energy commission for water regulation information.

☐ Contact water purification franchisors if interested.

☐ Contact plumbers for referrals.

☐ Contact your local water department about customer mailing.

☐ Contact office building owners, hospital chief engineers, hotel engineers, and purchasing agents for public buildings to tell them about your products.

☐ Write a business plan. Incorporate the knowledge gained from work accomplished on your checklist.

18

Self-Serve Auto Repair Garage

Tens of millions of dollars have been made by providing people with self-storage space. Metal storage buildings have converted vacant land with no cash flow into money-making developments. According to the National Apartment Association, sixty-six million Americans are renters. Many of these same people who desperately need a place to store their excess furnishings, boats, recreational vehicles, and other items have no place to work on their cars, motorcycles, lawn mowers, and gas-powered engines. There is nowhere for them to change their car's oil and spark plugs or to replace a battery. Although many people can afford to hire mechanics for all of their repairs, they would prefer to do the work themselves—if they only had a place to work or tools with which to do the work.

Talk to the owner of an auto parts store about a partnership. Your partner would contribute a full set of tools, repair manuals, and discount certificates for 10 percent off of selected auto parts. In return, you'd give the store owner a 25 percent interest in your company, which would be equitable.

After finalizing your partnership arrangement with a contract drafted by your attorney, you and your partner will need to rent two to three stalls next to each other. These stalls should be approximately 16' × 20', or 320 square feet in size. They should have adequate fluorescent lighting, engine hoists mounted on the ceiling, drive-up elevation ramps to raise the front end or rear end of the vehicle, a workbench, oil pans to collect the dirty oil, a full set of tools (etch your company name on each tool for positive identification), and a time clock. Depending upon where you live, these stalls should rent for $100 to $1,000 each per month. Obviously, there is an enormous cost difference between

Bismarck, North Dakota, and downtown Boston. Try to find stalls near other auto repair, body shop, or auto-painting businesses for your patrons' convenience. Be sure to have your attorney review your lease agreement before you sign.

If you rent the stalls to your customers for $15 per hour, you will earn gross revenue of $150 per day per stall, assuming you rent each ten hours per day. Three stalls would bring in $450 per day. If you rented the stalls only 50 percent of the time, you would earn $225 per day. Your stalls should be open seven days per week; thus, thirty days per month will give you a gross revenue of $6,750 per month just at 50 percent capacity. Subtract your stall rent of $300 to $3,000 and approximately $500 for part-time labor (assuming you don't want to work 70 hours every week), and you should net between $3,250 and $5,950 per month, depending upon your rent and labor costs.

If you market your business properly, you may be able to enjoy greater utilization than 50 percent and earn between $6,500 and $11,900 per month. For example, you could sell a block of time to nearby apartment complexes for use by their tenants at a re- duced price per hour or at no cost as a tenant benefit. Youth organizations, senior-citizen organizations, nursing homes, and condominium boards may all be interested in buying blocks of time for the exclusive use of their members or tenants. Your auto parts store partner should advertise a 10 percent discount to anybody who rents your auto repair stalls.

If you are not an auto mechanic, you may want to contract with one to act as a consultant to your customers for perhaps $20 per hour. The mechanic would pay you 10 percent per hour as a referral commission.

As housing becomes more expensive, Americans are looking for smaller, less expensive accommodations. Unfortunately, those living accommodations usually do not offer their owners a clean, suitable place to work on their cars.

Another, similar opportunity you may want to consider is open- ing a woodworking stall with accompanying storage unit for the carpenter who has no place to work. As I have said repeatedly, there are opportunities everywhere. Your task is to find the niche and exploit it.

SELF-SERVE AUTO REPAIR GARAGE
LAUNCH CHECKLIST

- ☐ Contact attorney about drafting partnership agreement and forming corporation.
- ☐ Open a checking account.
- ☐ Obtain IRS tax identification number from local IRS office.
- ☐ Order business cards, stationery, and brochures.
- ☐ Contact your insurance agent to obtain appropriate insurance coverage.
- ☐ File DBA if necessary.
- ☐ Negotiate part-time consulting agreement with auto mechanic.
- ☐ Obtain city business license if required.
- ☐ Contact commercial real estate agent about leasing repair locations.
- ☐ Contact owners of auto parts stores about partnership opportunity.
- ☐ Sell apartment complex managers, youth organizations, senior-citizen organizations, nursing homes, and condominium boards on concept and use.
- ☐ Write a business plan. Incorporate the knowledge gained from work accomplished on your checklist.

19

Parking Lot Striping

Sometimes the most obvious escapes us because it has always been there. The trained entrepreneur, like the trained detective, looks for clues and opportunities in obvious places. I know a man in Los Angeles who grosses over $500,000 per year painting the lines in parking lots that enable cars to park uniformly with a minimum of door smashing and a maximum use of every available square foot of parking space. Prospecting for business was simple. He read the new construction bulletins in his area. He drove around to examine the wear factor at existing parking lots. He found a number of hospital parking lots, county fairgrounds, and even a horse-racing track that painted its parking spots according to old standards. By reducing the size of each spot according to current standards, he increased the available parking by 4 percent. The extra 4 percent earned by the race track translated into $291,000 in additional revenue per year. Our parking lot entrepreneur charged only $210,000 for the entire job. He earned a net profit of over $130,000 for his three-week effort.

Getting started in this business requires very little investment. The essentials are a striping machine, paints, transportation, and money for advertising. Equipment such as that manufactured by Wagner (1770 Fernbrook Lane, Plymouth, MN 55447; [612] 553-0759) or Airlessco by Durotech Company (5397 Commerce Ave., Moorpark, CA 93021; [805] 523-0211) can be obtained from paint stores for approximately $2,400 to $3,500. If you're unable to locate a store that carries striping machines, you may want to contact the manufacturer directly for the name of a dealer in your area. There is no training needed and little maintenance necessary, and warranties are available for parts and servicing. The equipment is not extremely large but does weigh approximately 140 pounds, so it may be easier to transport the machinery in a truck or van. With latex traffic paint costing approximately $15 per gallon, it would cost around $300 to $400 to paint one thousand stalls.

Since requirements may vary by location, investigate the need to obtain a painting contractor's license and be bonded. In California, for example, a C-32 license is recommended; the cost is $300 plus bond. Also be sure to check your insurance needs, especially if you hire employees.

Just imagine, $500,000 per year with no limit to the opportunity; there are parking lots *all over the world*. You may even want to consider selling parking lot maintenance contracts that you and your attorney have drafted. Most malls require restriping at least every two years. For a flat annual fee you could agree to maintain the lines. Typically, $3.50 to $7.50 per stall is charged for brand-new lines (double-coated) and slightly less for restriping ($2.50 to $6.50), with some variation depending upon your geographical location. You can estimate approximately twenty hours to paint new stripes for one thousand stalls.

This is a great business because it enables you to continue working at your present job while earning extra money during evening and weekend hours. When the income from your line-painting business exceeds your regular income, you can work at it full time.

PARKING LOT STRIPING BUSINESS
LAUNCH CHECKLIST

☐ Form company.
☐ Open a bank account.
☐ Visit IRS office to obtain tax identification number.
☐ File DBA if necessary.
☐ Order business cards and stationery.
☐ Have attorney draft customer agreement. Try to obtain at least one of your competitor's agreements to make your attorney's job easier and save you money.
☐ Check with local paint store to obtain a bid on paint-striping machines and paint.

☐ Check with city to determine whether you need a business license and/or a contractor's license.

☐ Check with city to see whether a bond is required.

☐ Check with insurance agent about bond availability and cost. Also check on workers' compensation insurance if you intend to hire employees.

☐ Determine method of transporting equipment and paint.

☐ Write a business plan. Incorporate the knowledge gained from work accomplished on your checklist.

20

Compact Disc and Audiotape Retail Store

I am not a great fan of retail store ownership. The idea of buying inventory, renting space, hiring counter help, working long hours, paying high advertising costs, and dealing with the high probability that the business will fail has never really appealed to me. I owned a gourmet coffee store for five years. While the profits during the operating years were less than exciting, my payback came when I sold the business. Admittedly, some retail stores enjoy excellent profits, but retail stores are capital- and labor-intensive at best.

I've observed very little difference among most record stores I've visited. Placards describing the types of music and artists' names separate aisles of products; compact disc (CD) cleaners, blank tapes, and other audio accessories fill display racks; and employees staff the checkout counter. A few of the stores I've visited had expanded their inventory to include videotape rentals and sales. So why am I suggesting that you consider a retail CD and tape business? Because this particular business can be a real exception. It is in demand and it has great franchising possibilities and extraordinary profit potential.

Consider opening a store where customers can listen to the music *before* they buy. A counter in the rear of the store would have five or ten CD players, tape players, and turntables (for used LPs), each with a set of headphones for your customers' use.

You can also advertise for used CDs and tapes. In going through my CDs, I realized that I actually listen to less than 10 percent of them regularly. Many CDs in my collection were gifts, while others were purchased impulsively and without the benefit of being able to listen to them before buying them. How often I was disappointed when I got home. Many were played only once, and they just sit in my collection taking up space. Yet I can never recall taking a CD, tape, or record back to the store. (I still have records I purchased thirty years ago!) It would be great if I could sell these used CDs and tapes that are in good condition to a local music store. For my old LPs and tapes, I might receive $1 to $5 each, part in cash and part as store credit. Used CDs could bring up to $9. If I purchased a new CD or tape, the store could give me a slightly higher price for my old one as an inducement to buy more.

Trading in used CDs and tapes would create a unique resource and should draw music lovers from near and far. Your listening stations will encourage people to spend some time in your store, and because most of your customers will have already listened to the products they purchased, their satisfaction will grow while your returns diminish.

First decide what kind of atmosphere you want in your store and actively maintain it. Most of the audio stores I have visited blast incredibly loud music throughout the store. While the loud music may be a job benefit to the young, part-time high school checkout employee, it may discourage patronage by older people, who avoid noise pollution like the plague. Perhaps middle-of-the-road, softer (e.g., New Age) music would be more appropriate. With the headphones on, your customers can listen to music of their choice as loud as they want.

You may also want to consider opening a CD-*only store*. A $2.5 billion industry, CD sales continue to grow, outdistancing sales of long-playing records (LPs). And recordable CD players are still at least several years away from being marketed.

Or specialize in a particular type or era of music. But don't specialize to the exclusion of the music that would appeal to the general buying public.

Locate a shopping mall with heavy foot traffic and no direct competition. Ask the owners and managers of the mall stores about the landlord and lease terms, and attempt to find out what special arrangements they made with the landlord (if they will tell you). Observe the foot traffic for a few hours on weekdays and weekends to gauge potential sales volume. If a CD/tape store already exists in the location, chances are pretty good that the terms of the lease would prohibit you from getting a lease, since most malls give specialty stores exclusive tenancy.

Contact several CD and tape distributors in your area, and ask them about their products and discount programs. As a new store owner, finding a distributor who will really work with you is critical. Typically, distributors give retail store owners discounts of anywhere from 30 percent to 50 percent. Volume discounts of 1 percent and 5 percent also may be available. Once you establish credit, the distributor should give you thirty-day payment terms. You should expect to invest a minimum of $30,000 in inventory, $10,000 in display racks and counters, $8,000 in audio equipment, and enough working capital to finance operations for six to twelve months.

Your distributor can probably help you finance your initial inventory. He or she may also know of other stores going out of business that may have *used* display units, racks, and counters for sale. The distributor can also help educate you about the do's and don'ts in the CD business. Make sure that you talk to several distributors and wholesalers, and compare the information they give you. Be careful not to accept as fact what any one distributor or wholesaler may tell you, since each is trying to sell you his or her merchandise.

For this capital-intensive business, you may need to consider a Small Business Administration (SBA) loan or conventional loan from your local banker, but, as always, be careful when obtaining financing. The SBA and most banks will probably mandate that you personally guarantee any loan for your business. Resist giving a personal guarantee. Your business—including inventory and other assets—should be collateral enough. It is difficult enough pushing a business into the profit mode without becoming shackled to a large debt. Wherever possible, have your suppliers extend your credit terms to sixty or ninety days. Buy used equipment where possible.

You may want to present this unique business opportunity to investors and bring partners with capital into your company. Talk to friends, relatives, and business associates. Offer them a small percentage of your profits in return for precious working capital that will not have to be paid back until *after* you have become profitable.

RESOURCES

The Association of Retail Marketing Services
Three Caro Ct.
Red Bank, NJ 07701
(201) 842-5070

Billboard's International Manufacturing and Packaging Directory
Billboard Publications Inc.
1515 Broadway
New York, NY 10036
(212) 764-7300

CD *Review Digest*
Peri Press
Box 348
Voorheesville, NY 12186-0348
(518) 765-3163

Music and Sound Retailer
Testa Communications, Inc.
25 Willowdale Ave.
Port Washington, NY 11050
(516) 767-2500

Musician Magazine
Billboard Publications
33 Commercial St., #2
Gloucester, MA 01930
(508) 281-3110

COMPACT DISC AND AUDIOTAPE RETAIL BUSINESS LAUNCH CHECKLIST

☐ Form a corporation.

☐ Open a bank account.

☐ Obtain IRS tax identification number from local IRS office.

☐ Obtain resale tax permit from state board of equalization.

☐ File DBA with local newspaper if you elect to use a sole proprietorship or partnership instead of a corporation.

☐ Visit shopping malls and strip shopping centers to determine best location. Talk to owners of the malls and centers, and visit with merchants.

☐ Obtain city business license if required.

☐ Negotiate lease and have attorney review terms and conditions. Beware of triple-net leases and discuss alternative possibilities with your attorney.

☐ Obtain appropriate insurance coverage.

☐ Contact suppliers and negotiate supply contracts. Negotiate thirty- to ninety-day terms if possible. Try to get merchandise on consignment.

☐ Purchase display racks, counters, and fixtures if required.

☐ Sell stock and raise capital if not self-funding.

☐ Write a business plan. Incorporate the knowledge gained from work accomplished on your checklist.

21

Mobile Car Wash and Detailing

The increasing popularity of service businesses in the United States is being fueled by consumer needs. Because men and women are spending more time working and less time at home, they have fewer hours to devote to household tasks and chores. What little leisure time they have they want to enjoy, and washing the car isn't necessarily considered fun.

The International Carwash Association estimates that there are twenty-two thousand car washes (whether conveyorized full-service, automatic brush, or simply coin-operated self-service) in the United States. In 1988, according to a January 1990 *Motor Trend* article, the average car wash cleaned seventy-eight thousand cars. However, many people don't like subjecting their cars or recreational vehicles to automated car washes, since repeated exposure may damage paint, chrome, trim, and accessories. Others simply don't have the desire or time to drive to a car wash and wait in line. Even if you could find a drive-through car wash that isn't all that bad, wouldn't you prefer a professional mobile car wash that offers customers quality *and* convenience?

If you have a station wagon, small truck, or even just a large trunk in your car, you have what it takes to go into the mobile car wash business for yourself. Operating from your home, your expenses basically consist of your vehicle, cleaning supplies, and your telephone. Every motorist is your potential customer, and there should be plenty of repeat business, since cars continuously get dirty. In areas where bad weather is not uncommon, you can use your customer's carport, garage, or underground parking stall. You may consider driving your customer's car to your own garage, if necessary.

At your local auto parts store, buy some nonabrasive liquid

soap (preferably the kind intended for automobiles), two or three cans of auto wax, whitewall tire cleaner, several mitts or sponges, a couple dozen soft cotton cloths, one or two good tire brushes, one or two cans of chrome polish, and a twenty-five-foot hose with nozzle. The total cost should not exceed $100.

An alternative if your capital is not limited is to order a mobile car wash system from a nonfranchise business such as the following:

> Express Wash
> 908 Niagara Falls Blvd.
> North Tonawanda, NY 14120-2060
> (716) 692-4681
>
> Geo Systems
> 621 Lakeview Rd., Ste. C
> Clearwater, FL 34618
> (800) 237-0363
> (813) 447-7870 (in Florida)
>
> The Curtis System
> 9904 Mountain Rd.
> Box 250
> Stowe, VT 05672
> (800) 334-3395 ext. 9904

Prices for these supplies vary considerably. For example, Express Wash will provide start-up equipment, a marketing plan, a business manual, and ongoing support for approximately $1,750 to $2,100 (depending upon what system you purchase). Do some investigating before you decide to purchase.

Have your local printer produce one thousand one-color brochures that tout your auto-cleaning skills (I presume you have some), and you're working for the best boss in the world—*you!* Hand-distribute your brochures to doctors' and attorneys' offices, and don't overlook accountants, architects, and all the cars parked at country clubs and shopping malls.

You may offer to do the attorney's secretary's car at half price if the attorney has his or her car cleaned or detailed at the regular price. The doctor's nurse should be equally receptive;

nurses obviously don't make as much money as their bosses, but I will bet that they are just as busy. Your discount will encourage them to sell your service for you. Remember: everything in business is marketing.

Typically, you can charge $15 for a car wash including the interior. A wax and polish is worth $75 in large cities, and a complete detailing should command $95 to $115. You should probably establish a higher price for vans and trucks, since they will require additional time and supplies. One firm in Greenwich, Connecticut, charges $150 to $200 for its detailing service, which usually takes more than six hours. If a customer agrees to have you detail his or her car two or three times per year, give that customer a 10 percent discount. If a customer gives you three referrals, give another 10 percent discount. Word-of-mouth advertising is the best advertising in the world.

Schedule your car washes to minimize your travel time. For example, if you have five appointments scheduled on the south side of town, plan on doing them all in one day. After a while, you may have several scheduled in the same building, which will really improve your profitability. As time goes on and your clientele grows, you can add employees and really run the profits up.

Your earnings will depend upon what specific kind of operation you want to run and whether you hire employees or assistants. If you wash ten cars per day, you will earn $150 per day plus tips, or over $3,000 for a twenty-day month. If you wax and polish two cars per day and wash ten cars, you will earn over $6,000 per month, while you could earn almost $8,000 per month if you detail two cars per day and wash ten cars per day. That's a pretty serious gross return on a $100 investment. Of course, this volume of work won't happen overnight. But even if you cut the numbers in half, $1,500 to $4,000 a month is not hard to swallow while working out of your trunk! As your client base increases, you can hire employees to handle the growth and expand your customer base. Ten company-owned mobile car wash units would give you gross earnings of $15,000 to $40,000 a month.

RESOURCES

International Carwash Association
1 Imperial Pl.
1 E. 22nd St., Ste. 400
Lombard, IL 60148
(708) 495-0100

American Clean Car
Crain Communications Inc.
500 N. Dearborn St.
Chicago, IL 60610
(312) 337-7700

Auto Laundry News
Columbia Communications, Inc.
370 Lexington Ave.
New York, NY 10017
(212) 532-9290

MOBILE CAR WASH AND DETAILING BUSINESS LAUNCH CHECKLIST

☐ Form a company.
☐ Open a bank account.
☐ File a DBA with your local newspaper.
☐ Order business cards, stationery, and brochures.
☐ Purchase cleaning supplies and an answering machine since you will be working in the field.
☐ Obtain appropriate insurance.
☐ Check on franchise opportunities.
☐ Obtain city business license if required.
☐ Distribute brochures.
☐ Place advertisement in yellow pages.
☐ Write a business plan. Incorporate the knowledge gained from work accomplished on your checklist.

22

Seminars

Five hundred people, each depositing $20 at the seminar registration desk, marched into the Hilton Hotel ballroom in a large western city. Collectively, the attendees paid $10,000 to listen to this not-too-well-known motivational speaker, who gave a two-and-one-half-hour lecture on how to sell effectively. He made two presentations that day, two more the next day, and finally, two more the third day. He averaged $20,000 per day in entry fees, three days in a row, for $60,000 in seminar fees that week. He also sold audiotapes and videotapes. I estimate that he earned over $100,000 that week.

Of course, he had to pay approximately $5,000 for newspaper ads, $500 per day ($1,500) for the hotel auditorium, and perhaps $2,000 for the tape reproduction expense. His costs were approximately $8,500. Is it possible that he netted a pretax profit of $91,500? Yes, it is possible, and indeed he does so week after week after week.

Seminars provide a tremendous opportunity to educate customers or potential customers face-to-face. We see seminars advertised in the newspaper every day: Buy Foreclosures with No Money Down; Learn How to Prepare Your Taxes in One Day; Make Your Fortune in Real Estate; Learn the Secrets of Financial Success; How to Invest Your Money; Don't Pay Probate Taxes, Establish a Living Trust. Seminars provide easy-to-measure results to a much greater degree than most advertisements, trade shows, and direct-mail packages.

While some seminars are intended to make money through registration fees, others are designed to sell products or services. The one thing all seminars have in common is that they are designed to make a profit. Frequently they are used to establish a customer base for future seminars and other solicitations.

While some seminars are well thought out and offer the attendees true value for the monies received, others may leave you wondering why you wasted your time. The speakers who make money year after year do so by developing a seminar series with meaningful program content that offers value to its target audience. They perfect their presentation skills in order to produce positive results.

Each of us is looking for a way to succeed, a way to improve our ability to make money, influence people, and increase our self-esteem. In every field of endeavor, there are a select few who outperform their peers and become leaders whose expertise and counsel are sought by others. When you think about inspirational speakers, the names Billy Graham or Robert Schuller may come to mind. Zig Ziglar, Norman Cousins, Anthony Robbins, and Tom Hopkins may come to mind when you envision motivational speakers. Sam Gilbert, who figured out a unique way to acquire real estate, could have conducted real estate seminars and would have had standing room only. People would have paid Sam a lot of money to learn how they, too, could "make it."

Companies pay millions of dollars every year to send their employees to professional seminars, association-sponsored seminars, and self-improvement seminars. Executives pay $5,000 for one chief-executive training program in New York. I attended an excellent publishing seminar program at Stanford University and paid over $2,000 for the privilege.

Seminars can be a highly effective method of delivering a sales message. One of my most successful sales activities involved the sale of biomedical engineering services to hospitals. I tested hospital electronic equipment for electrical safety, but it was frequently difficult to get the hospital's chief engineer, administrator, and purchasing agent to participate in my sales presentation. I decided to organize an educational seminar to teach about the electrocution hazards in hospitals. I sent forty hospital chief engineers invitations to a six-hour seminar strategically located in a hotel in my target market area. Even though I charged a $100 seminar fee, sixteen engineers showed up, much to my surprise!

After hearing about specific electrocution hazards in intensive care, case studies of electrocution in hospitals, and the variety of dangers indigenous to the hospital environment, the chief engineers went back to their respective hospitals and relayed the information to their administrators. Shortly after the seminar, I had two major hospitals under contract and six sales pending!

Seminars can work if you properly target your audience. And once you've conducted several successful seminars, you'll probably find that you've gained additional credibility as an expert and are more sought after as a result.

Do you have a talent or level of expertise that people would pay to tap into? Do you sell real estate? Could you conduct a seminar on how to buy or sell homes? Are you a travel agent? How about a series of seminars on ways to travel inexpensively? How many people dread having to buy a car? Are you a good car salesperson who could advise prospective buyers about what to do and not do when buying a car? Each of these seminars could produce qualified leads and customers for the person conducting the seminar. Do you know of one salesperson who would *not* like to charge you money to have you listen to his or her sales presentation?

As an alternative to an expensive meeting hall, "cottage seminars" have proved popular for presentations that work better with smaller groups in a more intimate setting, like a home. A local interior decorator who gives seminars on how to decorate the home charges $50 per attendee, then shows the attendees fabrics, wallpapers, carpeting, and furnishings, which they may purchase.

Whether you are a motivational speaker earning $20,000 per day or a salesperson selling biomedical engineering services, seminars are a great way to effectively communicate with large groups of people. As a seminar leader, you have the audience's undivided attention and the opportunity to establish yourself as an authority on your subject matter. If you are relatively unknown, invite someone who is widely known, respected in the community, or an expert in a related field to join you in conducting the seminar or to endorse your seminar series.

Before announcing a seminar, allow yourself at least two to three months to work out the bugs. Begin by selecting the date and specific topic for your seminar. You may need as much as three months' lead time just to secure a conference room in a hotel, so plan ahead. Develop an advertisement to run in your local newspaper, making sure that you clearly state the purpose of the seminar and who should attend. Start a file of newspaper and magazine clippings of seminar advertisements that you think would attract the kind of audience you are seeking, and use these as inspiration for your own ad. Then outline your presentation and develop your slides, overhead transparencies, or other audiovisual materials.

You should also create some form of handouts for your attendees. These materials should include a questionnaire to be completed by the attendees at the close of the presentation; this instrument should be designed to elicit critical information about these potential customers as well as give you feedback on your presentation. You can follow up on this information with a phone call if it's appropriate.

You do not need a lot of money to launch your seminar business. If *you* do not want to spend the money to reserve a room, create and run an ad, or develop and duplicate your materials, *find a sponsor!* No matter what your subject matter, there are many potential sponsors. For example, if you want to give a seminar on interior decorating, negotiate with a local home-decorating store to pay for the seminar advertisements and local booking. In exchange, your sponsor can set up a display table in the back of the room and give a special 10 percent discount to all attendees on their decorating material purchases. If an attendee purchases a certain amount of materials, such a discount could actually pay for the cost of attending the seminar. An additional enticement to a sponsor could be a percentage of your registration fees.

One word of advice: it is best to keep your part of the seminar educational and minimize the commercial content and "hard sell," even if you are enlisting the support of a sponsor.

RESOURCES

American Society for Training & Development
1640 King St.
Box 1443
Alexandria, VA 22314
(703) 683-8100

Seminar Clearinghouse International, Inc.
350 N. Robert St., Ste. 598
St. Paul, MN 55101
(612) 293-1044

Seminar Information Service, Inc. (S.I.S. Database)
17752 Skypark Circle, Ste. 210
Irvine, CA 92714
(714) 261-9104

Seminars Directory
Gale Research Inc.
835 Penobscot Bldg.
Detroit, MI 48226
(313) 961-2242

Training Associates International
P.O. Box 1425
Ann Arbor, MI 48106
(313) 930-0880

The Training & Development Group
401 S. Milwaukee, Ste. 240
Wheeling, IL 60090
(708) 520-1155

Training
50 S. 9th St.
Minneapolis, MN 55402
(612) 333-0471

SEMINAR BUSINESS LAUNCH CHECKLIST

☐ Form a sole proprietorship.
☐ Design presentation materials.
☐ Have overhead transparencies and slides made.
☐ Arrange with hotel for a seminar room and audiovisual equipment.
☐ File DBA.
☐ Develop invitation list and forward invitations.

☐ Order business cards, stationery, and invitations, and purchase guest registration book.

☐ Obtain resale tax permit if you intend to sell products at
seminars.

☐ Negotiate sponsorship if applicable.

☐ Open a bank account.

☐ Obtain IRS tax identification number from local IRS office.

☐ Write a business plan. Incorporate the knowledge gained
from work accomplished on your checklist.

23

Import-Export

There are virtually thousands of products in this country that will probably never be sold in foreign markets. Of course, there are thousands—perhaps tens of thousands—of foreign products that will never find their way to our country. At a recent inventors' exposition in Houston, Texas, I saw a great ruler that was manufactured in Japan that took the guesswork out of hanging pictures. I also found a pair of ratcheted garden shears that had incorporated the concept of an auto jack in its design. With ease I pumped these shears through a piece of hard wood at least a half-inch thick. There were products from all over the world waiting for someone to bring them to market.

After discovering an electronic mosquito repeller at a business opportunities exposition, a business associate of mine began importing the devices for less than $2 each. He now sells hundreds of thousands of them on a national television home-shopping channel for $10. He literally makes over a million dollars a year in profits on *one product*.

Before you enter into any import-export project, you should ask yourself the following questions:

- What product are you interested in importing or exporting?
- To whom can you sell your product or service?
- From whom will you get the product or service?
- What changes are you going to have to make to the product or service so that it meets the cultural, technical, and quality standards of the country to which you are marketing the product?
- Does the profit margin make the transaction worthwhile?

Start simply by selecting one product to import or export that you either have experience with or understand well. You can find products at international trade shows, invention shows, business expositions, through friends, at work, or by traveling abroad. Once you've selected a product, you'll have to find a manufacturer that provides the product. If you have decided to export, find the appropriate *industry* newsletter, magazine, or association and start making contacts. If you are going to import and know which country makes your product, you will probably want to start your search for an industry contact at the office of the consulate closest to you here in the United States. Your next step might be to contact the country's international chamber of commerce. Other routes to take include going through the American embassy in the country or simply contacting the country's government directly. Most countries will supply you with a list of manufacturers in their country free of charge.

Once you have established the proper contacts, a visit to the country with which you intend to trade would be invaluable. If you wanted to import hypodermic needles from France, for instance, you could arrange through the French Consulate General's Office in Washington, D.C., to have a French government official meet you in Paris and escort you to all of the manufacturers of hypodermic needles in France. To encourage foreign trade, many countries will provide interpreters, transportation, and in many cases financing. For example, Ireland has earmarked tens of millions of Irish pounds to finance the export of the products made in that country.

To market your product in the United States, you could use manufacturers' representatives, wholesalers, trade shows, direct-mail campaigns, or direct sales. Internationally, you can also make valuable contacts at trade shows or through an agent who functions similarly to a manufacturers' representative.

It is extremely important that you have a solid team of professionals supporting your efforts. After researching various candidates in each area, develop a relationship with an international banker, a freight forwarder, a customhouse broker, an accountant, and an attorney well versed in international trade. Government regulations, tariffs, and tax incentives are factors in conducting business daily, so a strong support team is essential.

This is a business in which you will want to be especially detail-oriented and get everything in writing! Before you enter the international market, you might have to adapt your product to accommodate legal regulations as well as the cultural attitudes in the foreign market. Take into consideration packaging, labeling, brands, and trademarks. Specify the currency of payment where possible, and when importing make it a condition of your purchase that printed instructions, literature, warranties, and label copy all be printed in English.

When buying products from foreign sellers, you will probably be required to provide them with an irrevocable letter of credit issued by your bank in favor of your supplier. When your supplier gives the bank a bill of lading (proof of shipment), the bank wires your money directly to the supplier's bank. An irrevocable letter of credit is like a cashier's check held in escrow by a trustee. When the seller complies with the terms agreed upon, the money is released. Unless you have extraordinary credit, a bank will require that you deposit the money into an account before it will issue the letter of credit. In other words, you literally are paying 100 percent of your supplier's invoice before you receive the merchandise. It would be preferable if you could negotiate thirty-day terms after receipt of goods. When exporting, always insist on an irrevocable letter of credit in your favor. You do not want to be placed in the position of chasing a customer in a foreign country for payment.

The U.S. Customs Service will assess a duty on all imported items. As a rule, products that are not made in the United States usually have very small duties, while items that compete with American manufacturers carry heavier duties. For example, raw steel, automobiles, computers, and television sets have somewhat higher duties than certain pharmaceuticals and strategic metals indigenous to other countries.

Most major cities have customhouse brokers, who are in the business of clearing foreign products through customs for you. They will expedite the paperwork and payment of transportation costs, and they handle your ground transportation requirements. While their rates vary from city to city, you can expect to pay 3 to 6 percent of the value of your shipment for shipments worth up to $5,000. For shipments over $5,000, you will pay about half of that amount.

To determine what your opportunities might be, analyze what is going on in the world. For example, I know one businessman who read about the huge number of Russian Jews moving to Israel in 1990 and 1991. He knew someone in the portable/temporary housing business in Indianapolis, Indiana, and he negotiated a good wholesale price for the structures with the manufacturer. He flew to Tel Aviv, where he sold $40 million worth of temporary housing structures and earned $4 million for his troubles.

When you see something manufactured in the United States that is unique, functional, and has good perceived value, consider exporting it. I owned an interest in a Danish manufacturing company that produced wind machines that were used as an alternative source of electrical power. I sold as many windmills as I could manufacture to the California market at $150,000 each. When India literally shut the hydroelectric turbines off on the power going to Pakistan, I was offered $300,000 per turbine. In this age of global communication, international trade opportunities abound.

As a rule of thumb, I urge you to presell anything you are going to import or export. Do *not* buy products or build an inventory and then try to sell. Get a sample of the product to show to prospective buyers. If they take a serious interest in the product, take their order subject to reasonable lead times. This precaution will take a lot of the risk out of the transaction.

Another word of caution: If you are going to export to foreign countries, especially Second and Third World nations, you should know that bribes are a way of life. They are, however, still illegal in the United States. To make sure that you don't break the law, check with your attorney about the difference between commissions, fees, and bribes.

You can obtain the names and addresses of business brokers who can assist you in business in foreign countries. To do so, contact the United States International Chamber of Commerce and the office of the consul general for the specific countries with which you desire to do business.

There are fortunes to be made in importing and exporting, and it is still possible to start this business with as little as a $1,000 to $2,000 investment. Initially, you can set up your office in your home; eventually, you will probably need warehouse space for inventory and a larger office for staff members. Although the United States doesn't require any special license to become an importer or exporter, state and local licenses may be needed, and some foreign countries require licensing. Don't forget to contact your state's board of equalization about the need for a seller's permit. You may also have special insurance needs to consider, and a customs bond may be necessary. It's also important to make sure that your supplier has adequate patent protection before you launch your marketing effort, because there are a lot of knockoff experts who will steal a good idea in a second.

How would you like to be the importer of the next hot product like Perrier or Beluga caviar? Importing or exporting just one good product can cure your financial ills for a lifetime.

RESOURCES

American Association of Exporters and Importers
11 W. 42nd St.
New York, NY 10036
(212) 944-2230

Manufacturers' Agents National Association
23016 Mill Creek Rd.
Laguna Hills, CA 92653
(714) 859-4040

National Association of Manufacturers
1331 Pennsylvania Ave., NW, Ste. 1500 N
Washington, DC 20004-1703
(202) 637-3000

Sell Overseas America, The Association of American Export
2512 Artesia Blvd.
Redondo Beach, CA 90278
(213) 376-8788

International Trade Alert
International Trade Quarterly
11 W. 42nd St.
New York, NY 10036
(212) 944-2230

IMPORT-EXPORT BUSINESS LAUNCH CHECKLIST

- ☐ Meet with your attorney and form a corporation.
- ☐ Attend foreign trade shows and inventions conventions.
- ☐ Open a bank account and discuss letters of credit with your banker.
- ☐ Send letters to foreign agents in the countries where you want to import or export products.
- ☐ Obtain an IRS tax identification number.
- ☐ Find a good attorney who specializes in international business law to draft appropriate contracts.
- ☐ Obtain city license if required.
- ☐ Find a customhouse broker to handle the export and/or import of products for you.
- ☐ For an import business, contact prospective buyers of your products in the United States.
- ☐ Verify patent protection in countries where you intend to do business.
- ☐ Order business cards, stationery, and brochures if applicable.
- ☐ Talk to your insurance agent about appropriate insurance coverage.
- ☐ Write a business plan. Incorporate the knowledge gained from work accomplished on your checklist.

24

Silver Recovery

There are three legal ways to own the precious industrial metal silver: you can buy it, take it out of the ground, or recover it. It is used in x-ray film, standard photographic film, printed circuit boards and other electronic components, and a myriad of other industrial applications.

As with all tradable commodities, the price of silver fluctuates daily and is subject to supply and demand. If there is a greater supply of silver than demand for it, the price goes down. Conversely, if the demand is greater than the supply, the price goes up. Sometimes when speculators control large quantities of a commodity, they can artificially drive its price up. For example, when Bunker Hunt and his brother, Nelson Hunt, attempted to corner the silver market in 1980, it did not work, and they almost bankrupted Bache Securities in New York.

Futures trading is speculative; in other words, it is a financially risky business. If you buy silver outright, you will pay for the intrinsic value of the silver, a bar charge, and a commission to the company that is selling it to you. The market usually has to move up 5 to 10 percent before you break even, and, of course, there is no guarantee that it is going to go up. In fact, the market may go down. Then if you decide to sell your silver, you will have to pay a commission and restocking charge. So if you paid $5 per ounce plus a fifty cent surcharge, the price of silver dropped $1, and you decided to sell, the dealer would charge you another fifty cents to buy your silver back. You'd receive $3 for that same ounce of silver for a nearly 45 percent loss! If you put that same money in a savings account, you would have at least earned some interest on your money.

Mining silver is an expensive proposition and a bit risky. Because silver prices have dropped so low (below $4, in early 1991), it's difficult to find a silver-mining opportunity that is economically feasible. Although the cost of extracting silver varies considerably, for the sake of illustration, if it costs $6 per ounce to extract this precious metal from the ground but the silver brings only $4 on the open market, it's obviously better to leave it in the ground. In those rare instances where extraction does make economic sense, the capital required for exploration and mining is normally in the high six- and seven-figure range. The cost of silver mining is going up. Nearly all of the silver mined today comes as a by-product of mining for other metals, mainly lead, zinc, or copper. No new pure silver mines are being discovered.

Many photographic developing laboratories, small hospitals, medical diagnostic centers, and physicians' offices do not recover their silver from the developing solution. Others may use simple steel wool canisters to recover the silver in solution. You can buy inexpensive electrolytic silver recovery units for $500 to $1,500 (depending upon the unit size and the rate at which the unit recovers) from most precious-metal refineries and many photographic stores. If they do not stock them, they can usually order them for you. For additional sources of equipment, look under "X-Ray Apparatus and Supplies" in the yellow pages.

The equipment comes with simple installation instructions. Connect the input of the unit with the drain tube on your customer's developing processor equipment. Instead of the solution containing the silver going down the drain, it passes through the recovery unit, which collects the silver out of solution and allows the solution to go down the drain. Some developing processors come with an electrolytic recovery unit already attached.

The average two-hundred-bed community hospital produces 3,000 to 4,000 x-rays per month, which can yield as much as 100 ounces of pure silver. If you're recovering for a physician's office that has an x-ray machine, you will probably put a small recovery unit in the office. If you are recovering silver from a major hospital, it's probably best to use a larger unit. The amount of silver a hospital produces in a month is difficult to determine because of the number of variables. Only general medical x-rays can be used for silver extraction, and in recent years film manufacturers have decreased the amount of silver used in film.

ELECTROLYTIC SYSTEM

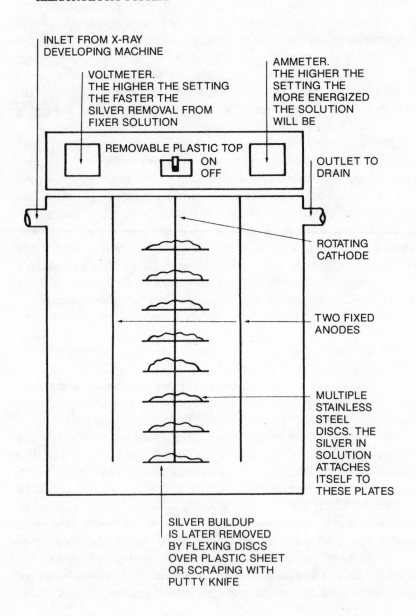

INLET FROM X-RAY
DEVELOPING MACHINE

VOLTMETER.
THE HIGHER THE SETTING
THE FASTER THE
SILVER REMOVAL FROM
FIXER SOLUTION

AMMETER.
THE HIGHER THE
SETTING THE
MORE ENERGIZED
THE SOLUTION
WILL BE

REMOVABLE PLASTIC TOP

ON
OFF

OUTLET TO
DRAIN

ROTATING
CATHODE

TWO FIXED
ANODES

MULTIPLE
STAINLESS
STEEL
DISCS. THE
SILVER IN
SOLUTION
ATTACHES
ITSELF TO
THESE PLATES

SILVER BUILDUP
IS LATER REMOVED
BY FLEXING DISCS
OVER PLASTIC SHEET
OR SCRAPING WITH
PUTTY KNIFE

Typically the silver recovery company gives the customer 70 percent of the silver recovered and keeps 30 percent as a service charge. Simply remove the silver in accordance with the manufacturer's instructions and any EPA guidelines and deliver it to a local precious-metal refinery. The refinery will charge you a small percentage of the gross weight to melt your silver down and pour it into good silver delivery bars. Check with the refineries to see if there is a minimum amount required for them to process your silver. You and your customers can take payment in cash or silver bars.

This is a great part-time business. The recovery machines are collecting silver twenty-four hours per day seven days a week, but removing the silver from the recovery units takes only fifteen to twenty minutes, and it's a lot easier than swinging a pick ax! If the price of silver goes up, you make more profit. If the price of silver goes down, you can take bars and wait for the price to go back up. If you buy the recovery units on time with your credit card or conventional financing, you can make the payments from your 30 percent revenue each month.

As time goes on, you may want to consider buying used, outdated x-ray files, gold and amalgam dental extractions, and precious-metal scrap from jewelry manufacturers.

Because the space in hospitals is so precious, you may wish to consider putting the x-rays on microfiche for the hospital. Most hospitals have to keep x-rays for at least seven years in case a physician or surgeon has to refer back to them, so hospitals often give the x-rays to a microfiche processor. The processor returns small file drawers of film for storage and future retrieval pursuant with the law. The hospital now has the use of all of that storage space for other purposes. The microfiche processor sells the film to the precious-metal refinery for a good profit. One entrepreneur processed seven thousand pounds for a La Puente, California, hospital shortly after the hospital filed for bankruptcy. He earned $90,000 in four days.

Opportunities abound in precious-metal recovery. There is a small company in Seattle, Washington, that strips old computers. The staff removes the printed circuit boards, gold-plated straps, rhodium-plated connectors, and other valuable parts, which are sold to a local refinery. The refinery strips the precious metals in acid baths, chemically removes the precious metals from the acid, and pours bars of gold, silver, and platinum-group metals. This Seattle-based entrepreneur gives his customers 50 percent of the precious metals recovered. All he needed to start his business was a pair of wire cutters and a screwdriver.

Visit a local precious-metal refinery and ask what materials you should remove from scrapped computers. Have them show you examples of desired material, so you will know what to remove. Talk to a local junkyard about buying the steel cabinets, chassis, and other nonprecious metals. You should be able to sell everything. All over the nation, no one knows what to do with all the used, obsolete computers—that is, not until they read this book.

RESOURCES

Silver Institute
1112 16th St. NW, Ste. 240
Washington, DC 20036
(202) 835-0185

Silver Users Association
1730 M St., NW, #911
Washington, DC 20036
(202) 785-3050

SILVER RECOVERY BUSINESS LAUNCH CHECKLIST

☐ Form a corporation and ask your attorney to draft a customer agreement for reclamation.
☐ Order business cards, stationery, and brochures if applicable.
☐ Obtain city business license if required.
☐ Open a bank account.
☐ Contact your insurance agent about obtaining appropriate business insurance coverage.
☐ Contact several precious-metal refineries and obtain competitive bids for processing your material and providing electrolytic recovery equipment.

☐ Investigate the cost and availability of a microfiche machine.
☐ Obtain an IRS tax identification number from your local IRS office.
☐ At a stationery store, purchase a customer receipt book, a scale for weighing materials, and plastic bags for separating customers' precious metals.
☐ Write a business plan. Incorporate the knowledge gained from work accomplished on your checklist.
☐ Distribute brochures and make sales calls on hospitals, medical clinics, physicians' offices, dentists' offices, and photographic processing laboratories.

25

Corporate Child Care

Two-thirds of the people entering the work force today are women, according to the Families and Work Institute. Of those women, 80 percent will get pregnant, and more than half of these females will return to work before their babies are a year old. In over sixteen million American families, both parents work and the children are age fourteen or younger. Over 7 percent of America's work force is mothers whose children are less than six years old, reports *Forbes* magazine (April 16, 1990). The simple truth is that in most American families today, both parents need to work for financial reasons. Large numbers of single parents are faced with the financial burden of supporting their families alone.

The common problem is how to care for the children when they are not in school and the parents are at work. The 65,000 to 70,000 child-care centers in operation today do not meet the high demand created by the socioeconomic forces at work in the United States. *Personnel Administrator* (April 1989) reports that of the twenty-five million children thirteen years old and younger, 5.5 million are cared for in another home, 1.5 million are in child-care centers, and 7.5 million stay in their own homes. The remaining 10.5 million have other arrangements, which include going to their parents' place of work when necessary.

According to a recent poll reported by *Personnel Administrator*, only 18 percent of working mothers were happy with their child-care arrangements. Parents are concerned about the availability, accessibility, and affordability of quality child care. Child care is increasingly worrisome as we read more and more about child molestation and poorly managed child-care centers. Approximately 94 percent of the family day-care homes are not licensed, but even licensed day-care centers are not above reproach. I read recently about a Midwestern center that was shut down by the state's licensing bureau for child-care facilities because the center was not providing adequate care; the children were found playing in their own excrement. If a child is too young for pre-school, the family may hire a sitter or a live-in au pair or governess, but this restricts the parents' privacy and is usually quite expensive.

Once the children have reached school age, the problems associated with child care diminish, or do they? The parent still has to get the child off to school. If the child gets sick or is injured at school, the parent usually leaves work, picks up the child, and takes care of the problem. In most cases the child gets out of school before the parent gets home from work. Unsupervised, latchkey children frequently find themselves in a great deal of trouble.

Improving child care is not an issue that only parents are concerned about. It has been estimated that absenteeism due to child-care problems costs American businesses approximately $3 billion each year. Along with absenteeism and tardiness come decreases in job productivity. Overtime to make up for lost hours is usually out of the question, no matter how important the business task at hand may be. Eventually, employee morale becomes low, and high turnover results.

About six years ago I was hosting a nationally syndicated television program, and my secretary and I were working on a close deadline to prepare for an interview with Howard Ruff on economics. My secretary was supposed to handle the airline reservations, hotel accommodations, script copies, and the shipment of the equipment for the camera crew. At exactly five o'clock, my secretary had to rush off to pick up her son at day care. She was unable to complete her tasks on time. The equipment did not get shipped. I ended up in a hotel thirty miles from the job site, and none of the scripts were copied. Without belaboring the point, let it suffice to say that there exists a crying need to improve on the child-care problem. Although the cost for such improvements may be high, we cannot afford to ignore the problem.

So what are some of the options available? Employers could establish a benefits plan enabling the employee to pay for child care (or dependent care) with pretax dollars. Or a company could offer a resource and referral plan to provide employees with the names of quality child-care facilities with openings. Emergency drop-in centers that are used when problems arise with routine child-care arrangements are becoming popular. Another alternative is a consortium child-care center that would allow a number of companies to share the costs and liabilities of operating a center. However, by its very nature, it may limit the amount of participation and influence of any one employer.

One answer is the establishment of a corporate child-care center. By mid-1989, about eight hundred corporations and hospitals already had established either on-site or nearby day-care centers (*Business Week*, July 10, 1989). The company allocates existing space in its building for a child-care facility to be run by a licensed and trained staff. Check with the state bureau in charge of licensing child-care facilities for the specific physical requirements of the interior and exterior space and necessary equipment. The center must be fully licensed, and the employer is responsible for physically developing the day-care center and purchasing any necessary equipment. Each employee using the center pays half of the weekly fee, and the company pays the other half. The company is reimbursed for the space and other allocated operational costs. So what is the business proposition?

Negotiate an agreement with an existing, licensed child-care center to staff and operate your corporate child-care center. Although you may not need to concern yourself with licensure, since your staff will be licensed, check with your city, county, and state bureau, because licensing requirements vary from state to state. The day-care center may still need to secure a license specific to your corporate client's facility.

Shop around and interview many prospective child-care centers. Prepare a list of suitable centers in order of preference, so that if your first choice does not work out, you will have alternatives. Inquire of the appropriate licensing board whether there have been any complaints about any of the centers on your list. Also check with the Better Business Bureau, police department, and the child abuse/neglect protection department, which is normally affiliated with the city or county social services agency. Get personal references on each center and visit the center unannounced to see the operation firsthand.

Once you have selected one child-care business with which to work, negotiate a low weekly rate per child. Now you're ready to talk to personnel department managers and owners of companies in your community about the advantages of providing child care on-premises. Greater employee satisfaction is a major key. Sarah Burud's Pasadena, California, consulting firm recently studied a child-care operation at Union Bank in Monterey Park, California. Her conclusions (as reported in the May 21, 1989, issue of the *Los Angeles Times*) included the following:

- The rate of turnover for employees using the on-site center was 2.2 percent annually compared to a 9.5 percent turnover rate for employees using other forms of day care.
- Mothers using the bank's day-care center came back from maternity leave 1.2 weeks sooner than others.
- Approximately 27 percent of new recruits said the day-care center was one of the main reasons they decided to apply to the company.

According to the Children's Defense Fund, the cost of full-time child care averages $3,000 per child per year, but costs vary widely. Let us assume for the sake of illustration that a parent is paying $125 per week for child care at an off-premises facility. You've negotiated a $90 weekly rate because the child-care center you contracted does not have to provide the actual facility, and you are providing a guaranteed minimum number of children. Your customer (the company) will have surveyed its employees about participation. You charge the company $150 per week per child for on-premises child care. The parent pays $75, which is a $50 savings over what the parent was paying. The company contributes $75 per child per week. For the company that is, of course, a tax-deductible contribution as an employee benefit. You pay your customer (the company) $25 per week per child for the use of the space and put $35 in your pocket per child per week. If you are taking care of ten children per week,

you will make $350 per week, or $18,200 per year. If you are
taking care of one hundred children per week, you will earn
$3,500 per week, or $182,000 per year.

One of the potential dangers is that the child-care center and
your customer could cut you out of the loop and deal directly
with one another. Have an attorney draft agreements for both the
company and the child-care facility. Make sure your customer
agreement prohibits the company from hiring your child-care
employees or entering into a contract with your licensed child-
care licensee for a period of five years after termination. You can
also put a noncircumvention paragraph into your agreement with
the child-care center.

This is a business with almost endless possibilities. Your
marketplace includes large hospitals, industrial complexes, major office buildings, large airports (for employees and visitors),
large hotels (employees and guests), major law firms, advertising
agencies, television stations, and large department stores. Talk
to unions in your community about including child care as an
employee benefit in their contracts. You, of course, would provide the service.

Prepare a concise brochure and print it in one or two colors.
Outline your program, describe the kind of professional staff that
you will be providing, state that you are licensed and competi-
tively priced, and list all of the advantages of a firm providing
child-care services to its employees.

If you can arrange to bill your customers weekly and pay your
child-care center on a net thirty-day basis, the business should
fund itself with positive cash flow. The key is to make your
customer pay you faster than you pay your supplier. If you achieve
this cash flow goal, your customers will be funding your business,
and you may never need to borrow money, pay interest, or
relinquish equity in order to raise operating capital. I know I
have emphasized this point elsewhere, but I cannot stress it
enough: good cash flow is second only to profits.

RESOURCES

National Association for the Education of Young Children
1834 Connecticut Ave., NW
Washington, DC 20009
(202) 232-8777

Child Care Action Campaign
330 7th Ave., 18th Floor
New York, NY 10001
(212) 239-0138

Child Care Information Exchange
Exchange Press Inc.
Box 2890
Redmond, WA 98073
(206) 883-9394

CORPORATE CHILD-CARE BUSINESS
LAUNCH CHECKLIST

☐ Contact attorney to form a corporation or general partnership with your child-care center as a general partner. Have attorney draft appropriate agreements.
☐ Contact your insurance agent about appropriate insurance coverage.
☐ Contact potential corporate clients and sell them on the concept and participation.
☐ Order business cards, stationery, and brochure.
☐ File DBA if appropriate.
☐ Contact child-care centers and negotiate agreement.
☐ Contact state to determine licensure requirements.
☐ Open a bank account.
☐ Contact IRS to obtain an IRS tax identification number.
☐ Write a business plan. Incorporate the knowledge gained from work accomplished on your checklist.

26

Public Relations

Do you have an outgoing personality? Are you good at organizing business and/or social events? Do you think you might enjoy working with the media? If you answer yes to one or more of these questions, consider starting a public relations (PR) company.

Large corporations, industrial firms, government agencies, hospitals, medical clinics, plastic surgeons, architects, publishing companies, travel agencies, charities, and even churches are just a few examples of organizations that need and use public relations firms to some extent. Law offices are hiring public relations firms to position them as experts in their area of specialization. Yes, movie and television stars, authors, and other celebrities still use public relations firms as well.

A recent *Wall Street Journal* article noted that in a softening economy, public relations agencies flourish because of PR's cost-effectiveness. In certain instances, public relations may provide a company or individual with more and better publicity than a paid advertising campaign. Phil Paladino, the publicist for Zsa Zsa Gabor, got more publicity for Zsa Zsa after she slapped a Beverly Hills policeman than most advertising agencies could probably have gotten for her for $5 million.

Let's take a hypothetical case. Assume you just invented a water-absorbing polymer that goes into the ground and saves homeowners or farmers 50 percent of their water usage. How could you most effectively announce the arrival and availability of this great product? You could allocate money for an advertising budget. With that budget you could buy advertising space in magazines and newspapers, purchase commercial time on television or radio, and rent booth space at lawn care and farming expositions. You could spend virtually any amount of money allocated. Or you could hire a public relations firm for a fraction of the cost. The firm could issue a press release and organize a press conference; arrange for radio talk show interviews, newspaper interviews, and magazine articles; and hold special events. The firm would book you or your company spokesperson on television shows, where you could demonstrate your unique product. You might wish to take a university professor or technical expert on the shows with you to lend credibility to the product.

One three-minute segment on "Good Morning America" or "Today" is worth hundreds of thousands of dollars in advertising, depending upon the show's actual Nielsen ratings. Moreover, when you appear as a guest instead of a paid advertiser, the station's endorsement is implied. Advertising professionals will tell you that implied endorsements are invaluable.

Media exposure is so important that Hill and Knowlton, one of the largest and best-known PR firms, uses its media training department to conduct mock television and radio interviews with its clients before the real thing. They videotape the mock interviews and critique how the client handles him- or herself, analyzing everything from the client's ability to think quickly to how he or she sits during the interview.

Although most of the employment opportunities are in larger cities, every community has PR opportunities. If a local medical clinic hires a new physician with a specialty greatly needed by the community, a welcome party may be in order. The public relations firm would book a room at a local hotel and provide hors d'oeuvres and cocktails to invited newspaper reporters, radio announcers, local television newscasters, hospital administrators, community leaders, and other interested parties. Upon arrival all attendees would receive a press kit that would consist of the following kinds of information: black-and-white photographs of the new physician and clinic; a history of the clinic, including its significant milestones; the new physician's curriculum vitae (resume), names of the physician's published papers and books, and his or her other noteworthy accomplishments; information about the physician's specialty; and finally an article about the news event itself.

Typically, a public relations firm meets with a prospective

client to get an understanding of his or her public relations needs. Whether a corporation's in-house public relations organ needs to farm out certain functions for a brief period of time or a company needs a full-blown public relations campaign designed from the ground up, a PR firm will estimate the number of hours required to prepare and implement a public relations program, then presents a written proposal to the prospective client.

Although the proposal may be project-specific and very limited in scope, usually the proposal will include a monthly retainer for the client to pay over a specified period of time. The PR firm may sometimes be able to bill its expenses on top of the fee, depending upon the scope of the campaign.

The major thrust for a new public relations program is normally concentrated up front and levels out over time. Usually the first step is to design, print, and distribute press kits and perhaps hold a press conference or media event.

Once a public relations firm finalizes the schedule and the client approves it, the PR firm basically manages the client's participation. The firm must make sure it understands the market it is addressing, the client's goals and objectives, and the likelihood of achieving them. The public relations firm takes charge and handles all arrangements for the campaign.

A standard PR program usually costs anywhere from $1,500 to $5,000 per month. A one-year minimum contract is often required. I know one Denver, Colorado, publicist who specializes in fashion PR and charges one fashion designer $16,000 per month for an all-encompassing PR program. She provides a great service because she knows *everybody* in the industry.

Because PR results are difficult to assess in many cases, the PR firm is often one of the first overhead items a company eliminates when cost reductions are mandated. Therefore, it is *essential* that you continually introduce your service to new prospective clients. Print your company name on all press kits and news releases. Distribute your business cards at the special events you organize, but try not to appear too opportunistic. The high quality of your press kits and organizational skills should speak well for your firm. Invite prospective clients to a seminar on the values of PR, which you host, or send out a press release if you land a big account.

Probably your best sales tool, however, will be the PR you've done for your customers. When competing medical clinics, hospitals, and physicians see what you are doing for the clinic that hired the new physician, they are going to want you to do the same good things for them. Be confident that each assignment will bring more work.

In PR, *contacts are everything.* Network with media people every chance you get. Join local media associations and go out of your way to speak with program directors, reporters, and key announcers. Since they need knowledgeable guests speaking on interesting topics, they need you as much as you need them! You probably cannot get the designer of a new bifocal lens on "Oprah," but you may be able to book the designer of a medical device that enables paraplegics to walk. A producer is constantly on the lookout for new ideas and different angles that will increase the show's viewing audience. The larger the number of viewers, the higher the show's rating and the more money advertisers pay. Greater advertising revenues improve the chances that the show will remain on the air longer and increase the amount of money the producer makes.

From time to time you will draft news releases and send them to your targeted market as well as to United Press International (UPI), a syndicated information-reporting service. Upon receipt of your news release, UPI puts it into their teletype machine and sends it all over the world to their thousands of newspaper, radio, and television subscribers. Usually only a few media subscribers will pick up your news item and use it. On rare occasions an especially interesting story will get picked up by a number of subscribers.

As a publicist, your job is to make the release as captivating as possible. If you're not comfortable with your ability to compose an exciting press release, a journalism class may help, or consider subcontracting the copywriting function to a professional. Unless you are an art director, you will probably also need to hire a freelance artist from time to time to assist in designing and laying out the artwork for press kits.

Some public relations firms employ over one thousand men and women and bill millions of dollars a year in fees. Most PR specialists, however, work either in small departments or alone. This is a business you can start in your home with very little initial capital and no full-time staff. In addition to taking courses in public relations at your local college, think about working for a public relations firm for a period of time before starting out on your own. As your own business becomes successful and the image of your company becomes more important, you may need to relocate your office to more elaborate surroundings. For working capital and cash flow purposes, consider incorporating your company and selling a small percentage of your stock to clients and potential clients.

This is a terrific time to enter this industry! Nationally, PR firms are reporting huge increases in business. Start-up companies are turning to agencies in great numbers, and there's an increasing use of PR by established corporations for crisis management and to improve corporate image. So the next time you see me on television talking about my book, you will know how I got there. Authors need a lot of help in the publicity department! Who knows? Maybe someday I will need to hire *your* PR firm.

RESOURCES

International Association of Business Communicators
One Hallidie Plaza, Ste. 600
San Francisco, CA 94102
(415) 433-3400

The Public Relations Society of America, Inc.
33 Irving Pl., 3rd Floor
New York, NY 10003
(212) 995-2230

Public Relations News
127 E. 80th St.
New York, NY 10021
(212) 879-7090

PR *Report*
Communication Research Associates, Inc.
10606 Mantz Rd.
Silver Spring, MD 20903
(301) 445-3230

Public Relations Journal
Public Relations Society of America
33 Irving Pl.
New York, NY 10003
(212) 995-2266

United Press International (UPI)
5 Pennsylvania Plaza, 16th Floor
New York, NY 10001
(212) 349-5310

PUBLIC RELATIONS BUSINESS LAUNCH CHECKLIST

- ☐ Form a sole proprietorship and have your attorney draft a client agreement.
- ☐ Open a bank account.
- ☐ File your DBA with a local newspaper.
- ☐ Set up an office in your home. To start, you should have an answering machine, file cabinet, small computer, fax machine, and desk.
- ☐ Contact local public relations firm about an apprenticeship program.
- ☐ Order business cards, stationery, and brochure.
- ☐ Obtain business license if required.
- ☐ Obtain IRS tax identification number from local IRS office.
- ☐ Contact potential clients and distribute brochures.
- ☐ Write a business plan. Incorporate the knowledge gained from work accomplished on your checklist.

27

Gold Panning

Gold panning may not be the most conventional business, but it sure can be one of the most lucrative. Lotteries and other legal businesses involving gambling frequently do very well during recessionary times. During the Great Depression numbers rackets flourished on the streets of New York and Chicago. It seems that the more difficult the struggle to earn money, the greater the temptation to win it. Owning and operating a gold-panning trough at a county fair is like running your own personal lottery. Every customer pays from $2 to $5 in hopes of finding gold that is worth much more.

Remember Tom Tilden in the chapter on consulting businesses? He cannot possibly cover all of the county, state, and private fairs in the United States. Don't reinvent the wheel. Duplicate what Tom is doing, and you, too, can enjoy the financial rewards that come from giving the marketplace what it wants: the chance to make a lot of money with minimal risk. Add to that the opportunity to learn a new skill and the enjoyment of participating in an almost forgotten art, and you have a winning combination.

Build a trough approximately ten feet long by two feet wide and one foot deep. As shown in the illustration, it should be V-shaped at the front end, so you can place a garden hose attached to a recirculating pump into it. The recirculating pump is placed in a twenty-gallon plastic container under the trough. At the other end of the trough, place a drain hose that drops into the same twenty-gallon plastic container. If you set up your equipment in this way, you can be completely self-contained and won't require running water to simulate a mountain stream. For less than $40, a good recirculating pump will give the effect you want with only twenty gallons of water.

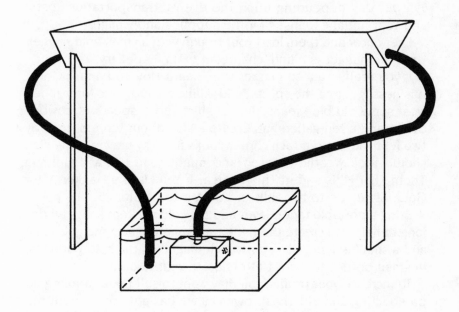

Coin dealers such as Continental Coin (5627 Sepulveda, Van Nuys, California 91411; [818] 781-4232), dealers of precious metals, and many gold refiners sell gold placer or nuggets. Some vendors may require that you purchase a minimum amount of gold, perhaps one-quarter to one-half ounce. To start, I'd recommend buying one ounce. Purchase your black plastic gold pans from Keene Engineering (9330 Corbin Ave., Northridge, CA 91324; [818] 993-0411) or another firm offering prospecting equipment. Small, ten-inch pans will cost about $2.50, while 17-inch ones are about $5.00 each. Instructions for use will accompany your pans. Buy a ten-pound bag of gravel, a ten-pound bag of sand, and ten pounds of medium-sized rocks. Add your gold dust, mix thoroughly, and pour the mixture into your trough.

You should add approximately one gram of gold dust per thirty pounds of gravel, sand, and rock mixture. At today's gold prices (approximately $500 per ounce), that will cost you less than $17. You can anticipate one hundred or more panners at $2 to $5 per chance to work to find the one gram in the trough. At $2 per try, you will earn around $175. At $5 per try, you will earn around $475. Of course, you will need to subtract your booth fee ($45 to

$95 per day depending upon the event), transportation costs, and your initial expenses for the supplies and trough.

Every now and then, load your trough with a small gold nugget. Until the nugget is found, charge an extra $5 per try.

If you really want to market the "Learn How to Pan for Gold" business, get into the spirit! To look like an authentic forty-niner, wear some old blue jeans, flannel shirt, red suspenders, cowboy boots, and a ten-gallon hat. Create a sign about ten feet long by two feet wide, and attach corner hooks for easy hanging. The sign should look weather-beaten and might read, "Thar's Gold in Them Thar Hills and in This Trough! If You Have a Hankerin' for Gold, Either Go to the Hills or Use My Trough for $5."

Bring a portable tape player and play old western songs all day long to help you create the right atmosphere. Place the gold dust and a small amount of water (which magnifies the gold particles) in small bottles to attract attention to your booth.

To increase your profits, you may want to sell books about gold prospecting and old ghost towns as well as gold pans (both the conventional metal type and the newer plastic type with spiral grooves manufactured into them to force the gold to settle at the bottom of the pan). Make sure you investigate the licensing requirements for each city where you have a booth. You'll need a sales tax permit for the sale of books and gold pans.

This is a great business that you can operate on a part-time basis while working at another full-time job. Use it to supplement your steady income until it becomes more financially rewarding than your full-time job. If you plan on having booths in several locations at once, try to enlist the help of relatives or close friends you can trust, since it's hard to police an employee's honesty in a business like this unless you are with that person at all times. Over time you'll be more experienced and will be able to estimate how many people to expect to pan for gold at your booth based on gross ticket sales.

Once you're up and running, work out real gold-prospecting trips to the California rivers and streams. In the Gold Country of California you should find promising streams near roads, resorts, and motels. *California Mining Journal* and the California Division of Mines and Geology are good sources of information. Before prospecting anywhere, check the ownership map at the county assessor's office so that you don't prospect on someone else's land without the owner's permission. Coordinate these mining expeditions with a local travel agency and earn 10 to 20 percent on each packaged price, including airfare, hotels, and ground transportation.

The gold-panning trough should work really well at fund-raising events and charity drives. You can charge a tax-deductible $10 to $20 per try and donate 50 percent of the revenue back to the charity. Your customer could write off half of the fee on his or her taxes. Contact hospital auxiliaries, fraternal organizations like the Masons, church groups such as the Knights of Columbus, and senior-citizen clubs. This could be a great money-maker for the Jaycees. And don't overlook swap meets as potential sites for your business.

You could also arrange treasure hunts with local radio stations and newspapers. For example, you could bury a nugget in a stream in or around your community, and the radio station and/ or newspaper would announce clues on a daily basis. The person who finds the gold nugget gets to keep the nugget and receives a prize from one of the participating sponsor's advertisers. You could personally announce the clues each day and remind folks to learn how to pan for gold at your booth. It's great advertising for you, fun for the community, and increases the listenership and readership for the media. Everybody wins! So how do you like the taste of stone soup?

RESOURCES

California Division of Mines and Geology
380 Civic Dr.
Pleasant Hill, CA 94523
(415) 646-5920

Gold Institute
1112 16th St., NW, Ste. 240
Washington, DC 20036
(202) 835-0185

Gold Prospectors Association of America
P.O. Box 507
Bonsall, CA 92003
(619) 728-6620

California Mining Journal
Box 2260
Aptos, CA 95001
(408) 662-2899

GOLD-PANNING BUSINESS LAUNCH CHECKLIST

- ☐ Form a sole proprietorship.
- ☐ Build your trough or have it constructed.
- ☐ Purchase the required equipment and supplies.
- ☐ Obtain a business license if required.
- ☐ Contact city, county, state, civic, and religious officials to obtain fair booth information and to book your preferred booth location. The best location is near the front gate or next to a food concession.
- ☐ Open a bank account.
- ☐ Obtain an IRS tax identification number from your local IRS office.
- ☐ File DBA.
- ☐ Order signage for your booth.
- ☐ Buy prospector outfit from western-clothing store.
- ☐ Contact travel agency to organize gold-prospecting trip to California.
- ☐ Obtain a resale tax permit from the state board of equalization.
- ☐ Write a business plan. Incorporate the knowledge gained from work accomplished on your checklist.

28

Auto Delivery

According to the U.S. Motor Vehicle Manufacturers Association, over 120 million cars and 50 million trucks were in use in 1988. What happens when someone with two or three cars is transferred to a new job in another state and can drive only one car to the new location? How do recreational river rafters retrieve their cars when they park their cars at one end of a river and then drift fifty miles downstream in a raft? What happens when a relative living across the country passes away and you inherit a car that you need delivered? How can cars be moved relatively inexpensively and efficiently in these situations?

Use an automobile delivery service. Delivery services are in contact with other delivery services in cities across the United States. When a driver delivers a car from Buffalo, New York, to Scranton, Pennsylvania, chances are pretty good that a car is waiting in Scranton to go back to Buffalo or some other city in reasonable proximity.

If a driver must fly back because a return vehicle is not available, the fee charged the driver increases to cover the airfare, calculated at the lowest coach fare with three to seven days' notice. Many auto transport companies allow students and other people to drive cars one way. It's certainly cheaper for them to drive across country than it is to fly or take a train.

In checking with auto transport services using car carriers throughout the country, I found that prices depend upon the size of the auto and distance of delivery. Door-to-door delivery charges are almost double those for terminal-to-terminal delivery. Charges for a vehicle the size of a Chevy Blazer, for example, are approximately $100 more than for a Ford Mustang in each instance. Moving companies frequently use such an auto transport service, or they move the car themselves on a flat open carrier with household goods or alone in a moving van. Alone in a moving van is considerably more expensive, however.

Typically, the mileage fees you charge your customer ($.20 to $.30) are twice your operating costs (insurance, fuel, oil, and administrative overhead). Initially you'll probably need ten on-call drivers, so I'd recommend using independent contractors. Pay them by the mile ($.10 per mile driven) and reimburse them for their expenses up to a designated daily rate. Thus, for every thousand miles driven, you should earn a gross profit of between $100 and $200.

It probably goes without saying that every driver must have a valid driver's license and good driving record, be bondable, and have no criminal record. Check with your attorney and insurance company to verify exactly what kind(s) of insurance your drivers should have. Retired men and women with good driving records are an excellent source of drivers. This may also be the perfect job for recent immigrants, a large labor market in certain areas of the United States like New York, Houston, and Los Angeles. Each must, however, have a green card or citizenship and a valid U.S. driver's license, speak English, and meet the other requirements just stated.

Initially, you can start your business from your home. Once your business gets off the ground, you'll need to open a small office with adequate parking space (preferably private, if it's affordable) nearby. Outbound automobiles will have to be parked for a period of time until drivers arrive, and there will be inbound cars waiting for owners. Once the owner has been notified that his or her car has arrived, charge a daily parking fee if the automobile is not picked up in a timely fashion. Your office should have standard office furnishings and a personal computer and printer for coordinating driving assignments, basic accounting, and record keeping.

In addition to advertising in your local yellow pages, have a descriptive brochure laid out and printed. The brochure should be distributed to personnel department heads at local plants and major companies. Also distribute your brochure to real estate agents, bicycling clubs, river rafting companies, governmental agencies, shipping companies, and customhouse brokers.

Automobiles coming in from foreign countries may need to be delivered from their point of entry. Automobile convention managers, military transfer agents on military bases, and movie production companies that move vehicles to remote locations should all receive your brochure.

Keep a running list of all of the recipients of your brochure, and follow up with a phone call. Antique automobile owners often need their automobiles transported to antique auto shows all over the United States. Purchase a list of antique car owners from a list broker, and mail them your brochure. (Most auto transport companies do not transport vehicles older than ten years unless they are antiques.)

Whenever quoting a job, compare the cost of using traditional moving methods by contacting the railroads and trucking companies to get their freight charges. In some cases, rail and commercial freight charges may be less than your fee. Classic car owners and owners of luxury cars may not want the additional mileage on their cars and may prefer to have a car transported by rail or truck. In these cases, you would arrange all of the details of the move and simply add a 50 percent carrying charge.

The insurance coverage is the automobile owner's coverage, and the transport company usually provides a limited amount of the deductible covered. In every instance, your customer should pay the estimated charge *in advance*. If that is not possible, charge at least half up front and require the balance upon delivery. I do not recommend that you extend credit to anyone. If someone fails to pay you, after due legal process, the automobile can probably be sold to reimburse you for your out-of-pocket costs. Once the car is returned to the owner, it could take you years to collect through the judicial process. If you accept 50 percent payment on delivery, then accept final payment by cashier's check only.

For your protection, have your attorney write a general contract for each customer to sign. Before transporting any vehicle, make certain that a current car registration is in the glove compartment and that the shipper is the person named on the registration. You don't want to be party to transporting stolen vehicles across the city or the country.

RESOURCES

Antique Automobile Magazine
501 W. Governor Rd.
P.O. Box 417
Hershey, PA 17033-0417
(717) 534-1910

Auto Transport Companies

All America Auto Transport
8929 Sepulveda Blvd., Ste. 406
Los Angeles, CA 90045
(800) 752-SHIP

American International Delivery
5250 W. Century Blvd., Ste. 714
Los Angeles, CA 90045
(800) 248-0054

AUTO DELIVERY BUSINESS LAUNCH CHECKLIST

- ☐ Visit your attorney to form a corporation. Have your attorney draft a customer transportation agreement.
- ☐ Check with your insurance agent about appropriate insurance coverage.
- ☐ Check with office leasing agent to rent space.
- ☐ Obtain city business license if required.
- ☐ Purchase office furnishings.
- ☐ Order business cards, stationery, and brochures.
- ☐ Order yellow pages advertisement.
- ☐ Distribute brochures.
- ☐ Open bank account.
- ☐ Obtain IRS tax identification number from your local IRS office.
- ☐ Contact other delivery services in other cities to develop cooperative program.
- ☐ Write a business plan. Incorporate the knowledge gained from work accomplished on your checklist.

29

Cooperative Purchasing

How much money would you have saved if you had paid 10 to 20 percent less for everything you purchased over the past year? If the average American household income is $30,000 per year after taxes, then the average family spends $30,000 on purchases. Assuming that half of the $30,000 is spent on mortgage or rent payments and food, then $15,000 is spent on other things. That means that the average family could save between $1,500 and $3,000 per year if they could save between 10 and 20 percent on their purchases.

People are searching for ways to stretch their dollars. Predictions for the foreseeable future are for continued slow growth in disposable income, and even in good times everyone enjoys a bargain. Every merchant wants to increase his or her business base and will do just about anything to encourage more customers, including advertising, promoting loss leaders, and taking risks by accepting personal checks. In your cooperative purchasing business, you will be giving each merchant a tangible way to increase his or her customer base, and the merchants, in turn, should be willing to give you a healthy discount on their products and services.

To start your cooperative purchasing business, have one thousand membership cards printed by your local printer. Because of the amount of information to be placed on the card, it should be a larger, folded business card. You should not spend more than $100 to $125 for one thousand one-color cards. Instead of having your name and address printed on the card, include membership information, as in the illustration. The back of the membership card would list the names of your participating merchants.

Individual memberships to your co-op would cost $24 per year,

(Front)

TOWNSEND MEMBERSHIP CARD

_____

Member's Name

Member Number 9620   Exp. Date 12-30-93

(Back)

Main Dept. Store_____	Tony's Barber Shop _____
Jim's Shoe Store _____	Denise's Secretarial _____
Harold's Bike Shop_____	Service
Jerome Smith, Atty. _____	Manfred's T.V. Repair_____
Dr. Milton Jones, M.D. _____	Tim's Dept. Store _____
Dr. G.J. Bye,	Accounting Services _____
Optometrist _____	Betty's Housekeeping _____
Audio Repair _____	American Architecture _____
Mercey Auto Repair _____	Phillip's Gas Station _____

with corporate memberships costing $500. Members receive a 10 percent discount at participating merchants' stores. Each merchant, therefore, charges your members 90 percent of the retail price and nets only 80 percent from each sale because he or she must also pay *you* 10 percent of the retail price. You may need to negotiate the merchant's percentage, since this arrangement may be too high for some firms.

So, you say, "Great idea, Chuck, but how do I monitor the member's use of his membership card? After all, the participating merchants are collecting 90 percent of the retail price, and I am asking them to turn 10 percent of the money they collect over to me." That's a good question, one that took some time for me to answer. Of course, you can always introduce electronic equipment that would be used in conjunction with an issued membership card, but that is expensive to buy, install, maintain, and monitor. Another alternative would be to issue a multipart form to each merchant and have each member's purchase written up on the special form. But the merchant could forget to use it or may be unwilling to use it because the store's existing sales order form must be used because of current systems.

I suggest that each merchant be given a special stamp engraved with the store's initials. Each time a member makes a purchase, the merchant would stamp the membership card and write down the dollar value of the purchase. The back of a completed card would look like this example:

MOS 42.00	PTL 12.18	LLL 15.00	CRW 14.18
GJB 72.16	JJM 52.60	TPQ 263.00	CHS 81.00
MAR 116.30	PMJ 16.00	SWR 207.00	DAW 6.52

At the end of every month, the members would mail in or bring in their cards. Upon receipt of the old card, a new one would be sent to the member. The member who used the membership card the most would receive an additional 5 percent discount (from your 10 percent) in the form of a cash rebate for all of last month's purchases. This incentive should encourage your members to send in their cards. The fact that the cards are only good from month to month will also encourage the return of the cards that have been filled out.

At the end of each month, you would total the dollar volume for each merchant, multiply that number by 10 percent, and pick up your checks. If you had five hundred members purchasing an average of $500 per month, the gross purchasing power of your cooperative purchasing company would be one-quarter of a million dollars per month. Your 10 percent would net you $25,000 per month.

Some senior-citizen clubs have over 500 members in larger cities. Engage your local teachers association, Optimist Club, Jaycees, postal workers, trade unions, the sheriff's department, and other organizations to use your membership card, and have personnel managers distribute them to employees. Five hundred members is not unrealistic. Many cooperative purchasing organizations have tens of thousands of members.

You may want to consider forming a corporation and selling a small percentage of stock to finance your start-up expenses. You will need money to open an office and pay your attorney, accountant, and printer. You will also need money to live on, as it will probably take from six months to a year before you will recognize any substantial profit from which you can reasonably anticipate a salary. Minimally, you should have $1,000 to $25,000 available to you, depending on the growth projections you've outlined in your business plan.

You may want to consider cooperative purchasing businesses for churches, hospitals, landscape companies, and restaurants. Every industry that buys products and services can benefit from participating in a cooperative purchasing program. Individually they may not qualify for maximum discounts based upon high-volume purchases. If you can buy for five, ten, or one hundred similar businesses, you can probably negotiate deep discounts and pass 50 percent of your discount on to the participating members. You would make a handsome profit, and your members would save a significant amount of money on their purchases. This can be an extremely lucrative business for a hard-working entrepreneur.

RESOURCES

National Association of Accountants for Cooperatives
6320 Augusta Dr., Ste. 800
Springfield, VA 22150
(703) 569-3088

National Association of Co-op Advertising
1200 McArthur Blvd.
Mahwah, NJ 07430
(201) 327-2667

Merchandise Trends
425 Park Ave.
New York, NY 10022
(212) 371-9400

COOPERATIVE PURCHASING BUSINESS
LAUNCH CHECKLIST

- ☐ Form a corporation.
- ☐ Open a bank account.
- ☐ Order business cards, stationery, and brochures.
- ☐ Obtain an IRS tax identification number from your local IRS office.
- ☐ Obtain city business license if required.
- ☐ Have attorney draft the merchant agreement and the member agreement.
- ☐ Raise required capital if not self-funded.
- ☐ Set up office with small computer, desk, file cabinet, answering machine, and fax machine.
- ☐ Distribute brochures.
- ☐ Contact potential membership groups.
- ☐ Contact merchants about program participation.
- ☐ Order membership cards.
- ☐ Write a business plan. Incorporate the knowledge gained from work accomplished on your checklist.

30

Special Janitorial Service

Some janitorial service companies service homes, while others service offices, banks, industrial sites, and theaters. I know one company that specialized in model home and model apartment cleaning for contractors and apartment building owners. Another does move-in/move-out cleaning for real estate offices, cleaning homes and apartments before the next renter or owner moves in. Some serve all of these customers, as well as anybody else who wants his or her home cleaned.

You may have guessed by now that I found a niche and opened my own janitorial service, one of my most profitable businesses. What type of business can you think of that needs janitorial cleaning as much or more than any other business, yet hesitates to hire a janitorial service company? The answer is jewelry manufacturers and companies that manufacture products that use precious metals. Just imagine thirty workstations with employees grinding, filing, and polishing gold, silver, and platinum jewelry. Once airborne, the microscopic dust particles end up on window ledges, in cracks in the floors, embedded in the carpeting, and in door jambs and wall crevices.

If you are willing to grow slowly, you can do all of the cleaning yourself and even start on a part-time basis. Eventually, you can hire one or two part-time helpers. I paid my part-time employees minimum wages with a 5 percent "precious metals recovered" incentive. Meticulous work habits reap substantial rewards in this business. All you need to get started is a vacuum cleaner and bags, rubber aprons and gloves, wire brushes, metal containers, small whisk brooms, and dusting cloths. (Due to the nature of this particular niche, you'll need to continually replace the vacuum bags and cleaning cloths.) On occasion you may need to have some basic hand tools available so you can lift up carpeting.

Although your brochures and yellow pages ads may bring in customers, you should identify potential customers in the "Jewelry Manufacturing" section of the yellow pages. The greatest concentrations of jewelry manufacturers are in Los Angeles, Montreal, and New York, but if you don't live in one of those cities, do not be discouraged. Many geographic areas have unique markets and manufacturing facilities.

After you've identified your potential customers, visit each and ask to bid on a cleaning contract. Present each a formal, written bid showing a breakdown of charges and why the company should elect to do business with your firm. To arrive at your bid, consider square footage, time necessary for cleaning, extra supplies, staffing costs, special cleaning needs, and your profit. Once your bid is accepted, ask your customer to sign a maintenance agreement drafted by your attorney that sets forth what services you'll provide, the frequency of service, terms of payment, and other items your attorney feels are necessary.

When you and your crew arrive at the job site, your workers should put on rubber aprons and gloves; upon leaving, the aprons and gloves can be washed with a cleaning cloth, and the cloths can be placed in the metal container for precious-metal recovery. Wipe down everything, including workstations, bathrooms, offices, window ledges, and windowsills. If the customer uses a vacuum collection system, clean the system thoroughly. Replace old vacuum bags with clean ones. Vacuum the floors thoroughly. Use the wire brush on cracks in wooden floors and between tiles where applicable. If your customer will allow you to remove old carpeting, outdated drapes, and curtains, do so. The precious metal recovered may provide the customer with enough cash to buy new ones and still have money left over. Of course, all of the rags, vacuum bags, rugs, paper towels, and even drapery will be burned by your refiner.

Most major cities in the United States have precious-metal refineries. A precious-metal refinery processes precious-metal-containing materials and pours finished gold, silver, and platinum ingots. For example, if you had a barrel full of dust cloths with gold dust in them, the refinery would burn them and melt down the metal left after burning. After meltdown, they would pour a fine gold bar. You could take the gold bar or have the refinery buy it from you at the settlement date price (since precious-metal prices fluctuate daily). You would then pay your customer 50 percent of the recovered amount.

I negotiated a fifty-fifty split with my customers. Some jobs paid me a modest return, while others were downright phenomenal. One jewelry manufacturer in Honolulu, Hawaii, had been making gold chains and rings for over twenty-five years. His carpets had not been cleaned for *years*. When we lifted the carpet, we found gold dust embedded in the mat under the wall-to-wall carpets. The refinery processed over twenty-five ounces of gold for that one jeweler. Gold was selling for $800 per ounce at the time. The jeweler was pleased to receive $10,000 and I was more than pleased to receive my $10,000 share (25 ounces $\times$ $800 = $20,000, or $10,000 each). Not many janitorial cleaning companies earn $10,000 in one day. Of course, the refinery is going to charge you a nominal processing charge, and you have to pay your part-time help their wages and commissions. Still, an $8,000 net check is a good day's work by most standards.

There are other niche opportunities in the janitorial business. You could specialize in cleaning physicians' and dentists' offices, and clean their instruments and patient areas with special antiseptic cleaning materials. Once you're up and running, you may want to add other specialized services to improve profits and demonstrate that your firm can successfully perform a variety of services. If you consider all of the possibilities and find a group of potential customers with unique needs that are probably not being met, you have a great business opportunity.

RESOURCES

Building Service Contractors Association
10201 Lee Hwy., Ste. 225
Fairfax, VA 22030
(800) 368-3414

Jewelry Industry Distributors Association
720 Light St.
Baltimore, MD 21230
(301) 752-3318

National Housekeepers Association
1001 Eastwind Dr., Ste. 301
Westerville, OH 43081
(614) 895-7166

Building Services Contractor
445 Broad Hollow Rd., Ste. 21
Melville, NY 11747
(516) 845-2700

Sanitary Maintenance Magazine
2100 W. Florist
Milwaukee, WI 53209
(414) 228-7701

Services Magazine
10201 Lee Hwy., Ste. 225
Fairfax, VA 22030
(800) 368-3414

SPECIAL JANITORIAL SERVICE LAUNCH CHECKLIST

☐ Form a corporation.
☐ Open a bank account.
☐ Obtain an IRS tax identification number from IRS office.
☐ Order business cards, stationery, and brochures.
☐ Obtain city business license.
☐ See your attorney about drafting a customer agreement.
☐ Meet with your insurance agent to obtain appropriate insurance coverage.
☐ Contact a precious-metal refiner about processing your scrap material.
☐ Purchase the required equipment and supplies.
☐ Sell your specialized cleaning service to your niche market.
☐ Write a business plan. Incorporate the knowledge gained from work accomplished on your checklist.

31

Carpet Cleaning

One of my best friends, Roger Abdo, has been cleaning carpets and upholstery since 1950. Roger takes great pride in his work. He has never advertised. He has never employed a salesperson. Yet Roger has made a very good living because he believes he has no real competition: "The margin between being good at your work and doing an excellent job can be small. Excellence is the key, and that's your best advertisement."

While Roger's work crew aggressively moves furniture, mixes the cleaning solvents, and begins the cleaning process, Roger frequently spends time with the customer to determine whether the customer has any special needs beyond the basic task at hand. He evaluates any troublesome spots or stains, high-traffic wear-and-tear areas, and badly worn carpet, and he lets his customers know if there are any stains that probably won't come out or if there are areas that may need special treatment. Everything is done according to specifications. Roger guarantees satisfaction with his work and phones his customers within a couple of days following the job to see if the job is still satisfactory.

Roger's referral business is one of the best I have ever seen. One day he is cleaning a minister's carpets at his home; the next day he is cleaning the church's carpets. One day he is cleaning carpets at a movie studio, and then he finds himself cleaning a celebrity's carpets the following week. Although his rates are 20 to 30 percent higher than some of his competitors', Roger is booked months ahead.

How does he do it? His outstanding performance, strong customer service attitude, and hard work place him above his competitors. Not head and shoulders above, but enough to cross the line into the category of excellence. Sometimes horses win only by a nose, but it's enough to ensure a trip to the winner's circle. Often the difference between a mediocre business and one that provides its owner with financial independence is that little extra effort.

Why should you consider carpet cleaning? Compared to many businesses, the start-up costs are low, you can work out of your home, it's nonseasonal, and it's a growing industry. Basically, you'll need cleaning equipment, cleaning supplies, one assistant, and a method of transportation for you and your equipment. If economically possible, you may wish to serve an apprenticeship with a reputable, established firm in order to get some valuable experience under your belt.

Your market is composed of the millions of homes, offices, and specialty buildings that are carpeted. The average homeowners have their carpets cleaned every one and a half to two years; businesses will usually require more frequent cleanings. What you'll find is that carpet cleaning is an educational process for the customer; once your customers can see how well the cleaning can be done and how much better their carpets look, they'll be repeat customers.

Some carpet cleaners will quote a price by the room, while others quote by the square foot. Generally, you should interview a new customer over the phone; determine his or her cleaning needs, type of carpet or upholstery, average room size(s); and give an estimate before arriving at the scene where you can firm up the quote just before performing the actual work. At an average cost of sixteen to twenty cents per square foot for unfurnished areas or twenty to twenty-four cents per square foot for furnished rooms, this is a multibillion-dollar industry.

Some carpet-cleaning companies offer inexpensive steam cleaning for the lower-end market. Others who offer a specialized chemical treatment cleaning will advertise that the cost is higher but the results make the extra cost worthwhile. There are companies that clean only Oriental rugs. Some firms specialize in upholstery cleaning, and some clean only auto upholstery. Entrepreneurs will look for niches in existing markets, and carpet cleaning is no exception. Who would you rather have service your Chevrolet truck—a Chevrolet mechanic who works only on Chevrolets, or a garage mechanic who works on any and all vehicles? With few exceptions, the specialist is your best bet. Remember: specialization sells.

A new carpet-cleaning franchise can cost anywhere from $5,000 to $25,000, while purchasing an existing business or franchise will generally cost you much more. For anywhere from $15,000 to $25,000, you can buy a franchise from a company such as Chem-Dry, and they will provide you with a territory, cleaning equipment, ongoing training, financing, and marketing support. They have been franchising for fourteen of their eighteen years in business. Other companies such as Professional Carpet Systems offer a franchise for about $5,000, which includes your territory, training, and support; your out-of-pocket expenses of approximately $8,500 purchase your equipment, chemicals, and dyes. Although only 25 percent of Professional Carpet Systems' work is dyeing carpets, this accounts for approximately 50 percent of their revenues. Some of these franchises get well over $65,000 in their first year of operation.

At the other end of the spectrum, you can buy a good portable cleaning system for $2,000 to $3,000, put it in the back of a station wagon or van, and you are off to the races. Check with other carpet-cleaning companies for recommendations about specific manufacturers and types of equipment to best suit your needs. Before you purchase, be sure to investigate your options: the availability of training, equipment warranties, rebuilt or secondhand equipment, rental or lease options. Usually equipment manufacturers are willing to train their customers in how to use their equipment and cleaning supplies.

Word of mouth is probably your best advertisement. Although most cleaning companies do advertise, they are divided about the return on their ad dollar investments. Make sure that you are listed in all of the yellow pages in your area. Since you are in a start-up situation, if your budget allows, you may wish to advertise your carpet-cleaning service in local newspapers, or you may decide to have an inexpensive one-color door hanger ad printed. When you're not cleaning carpets, hang the door hanger advertisements on front doorknobs.

If you want to keep your initial costs down, contact real estate sales managers in your area and offer them a 10 percent referral fee for leads. Many people listing their homes want their carpets cleaned to help in selling their property. Also, many Realtors manage apartment complexes and condominiums. When a tenant moves out, the tenant's cleaning deposit is often used to pay for carpet cleaning. Initially you may also want to promote your work with before-and-after photos that you've taken of previous jobs. Don't overlook the value of commercial accounts such as office buildings, hospitals, and the like. After proving that your work and service are exceptional and a good value, try to obtain a long-term contract with the building management. Offer a slight discount if they agree to monthly services of a certain dollar amount or agree to include upholstery in addition to carpet-cleaning services (if you have expanded into that field).

To be thorough, most carpet-cleaning jobs will require at least two people. Furniture frequently must be moved and placed on plastic tabs to prevent rust or stain marks, and your equipment must be moved. Increase your income by adding personnel. Expect to pay each employee an hourly wage of $5 to $10; you might wish to query other carpet cleaners in your area to establish a fair, competitive wage for the work. More experienced employees who are capable of supervising jobs themselves should receive a higher hourly wage and perhaps even commissions as well. Make sure you comply with all state and federal guidelines for compensation, withholding, worker's compensation, and the like. You'll also need to talk with your insurance agent about a general liability insurance policy.

A great way to build your new business would be to give each of your customers a 5 percent discount on his or her next cleaning job for each new referral that turns into a job for you. Don't limit the number of names and phone numbers each gives you. Contact these referrals, telling each person on the list who asked you to call. If twenty referrals give you a job, you would clean the original referring customer's carpet *for free*. New customers will in turn give you referrals. By the end of the first year, you will have hundreds if not thousands of potential new customers.

There are many carpet-cleaning companies, and the consumer may have a difficult time deciding who to call. But remember that you can attain financial independence by providing special, exceptional service.

RESOURCES

Carpet & Rug Institute
P.O. Box 2048
Dalton, GA 30722
(404) 278-3176

Professional Cleaning Journal
2626 Valley View Lane, Ste. 11
Dallas, TX 75234
(214) 484-4474

Installation & Cleaning Specialist
17835 Ventura Blvd.
Encino, CA 91316
(818) 345-3550

Manufacturers

The Butler Corporation
251 Moody St.
Ludlow, MA 01056
(800) 535-5025
(413) 547-8557 (in Massachusetts)

Chem-Dry
Harris Research, Inc.
3330 Cameron Park Dr., Ste. 700
Cameron Park, CA 95682
(800) 841-6583
(800) 821-3240 ext. 7000 (in California)

HydraMaster
20309 64th Ave. W.
Lynnwood, WA 98036
(800) 426-1301
(206) 775-7272 (in Washington)

Professional Carpet Systems
5182 Old Dixie Hwy.
Forest Park, GA 30050
(800) 735-5055
(404) 361-9362 (in Georgia)

Steam Genie
8613 Aviation Blvd.
Inglewood, CA 90301
(800) 345-2411
(213) 776-2411 (in California)

U.S. Products, Inc.
North 10450 Airport Dr.
Hayden Lake, ID 83835
(800) 257-7982
(208) 772-0573 (in Idaho)

CARPET-CLEANING BUSINESS LAUNCH CHECKLIST

☐ Form a company.
☐ Open a bank account.
☐ File DBA with local newspaper.
☐ Order business cards and stationery.
☐ Obtain city business license if required.
☐ Visit local IRS office to obtain your IRS tax identification number.
☐ Check with your insurance agent about a general liability policy.
☐ Check with other carpet-cleaning firms in your community for equipment suggestions and possible apprenticeship opportunities.
☐ Check on carpet-cleaning franchises.
☐ Have simple doorknob advertisements printed.
☐ Contact real estate office managers to offer referral commissions and discounts on property that they manage.
☐ Write a business plan. Incorporate the knowledge gained from work accomplished on your checklist.

32

Retail Store for Senior Citizens

Since senior citizens promise to be one of the hottest markets of the decade, this may well be *the* niche business of the nineties. With the graying of America, these seniors are the fastest-growing segment of the nation's population, in addition to representing 75 percent of the nation's wealth. By the year 2000, senior citizens will account for approximately 13 percent of the U.S. population. By the middle of the next century, one in five persons will be age sixty-five or older.

What do senior citizens need? They are often living on fixed incomes, and as inflation marches on, eroding the value of the dollar, there are no wages to follow. Wage earners, on the other hand, often keep their heads above water. As inflation goes up, their salaries go up, and their buying power remains a relative constant. In other words, if you are earning $2,000 per month and paying $1,000 per month on rent, 50 percent of your income is going toward rent. If five years later you are earning $4,000 per month and paying $2,000 per month for rent, you are still contributing 50 percent of your income to rent. If you are retired and must rely on Social Security and interest income, you would probably be in serious trouble if your fixed income totaled $2,000 and your rent went from $1,000 to $2,000 in five years; there would be no money left for food, clothes, medical care, and other necessities.

According to Ken Dychtwald, author of *Age Wave*, more than 85 percent of American men and women age fifty-five and older do not work. Therefore, filling up their time is a major concern for seniors. Also extremely important is finding businesses to help them save and manage their money. Retail merchants, physicians, opticians, accountants, rental agents, nursing homes, hospitals, and a host of service agencies want the seniors' business, and they are frequently willing to pay a referral fee to get it. Moreover, they are usually happy to offer special discounts to senior citizens.

In this business your role is to serve as an information resource and service coordinator. A senior citizen could visit your store and pick up applications for various low-income housing, governmental income-subsidy programs, county welfare programs, and community-sponsored meal delivery services. Find out about job opportunities in the area from your state employment office, and present job-training program opportunities offered by local vocational schools. You could offer referrals to eyewear stores, travel agencies, medical facilities, legal specialists, pharmacies, dry cleaners, shoe repair shops, and other businesses.

Obviously, people could get the same information from the yellow pages or by phoning friends or relatives. But you'll have all the information in one place for their convenience and can even help them decide which one to use. By doing a little comparison shopping, you'll be able to suggest two or three alternatives offering the best price, best service, and fastest service.

How do seniors find a bridge club, ski club, chess club, shopping club, or community center to join? Through you. You can also organize social events at your center for a small fee (perhaps $2). On Monday nights, hold dances for seniors; on Tuesday nights, hold Scrabble contests. On Wednesday nights, sponsor cooking classes at a local kitchenware store, while Thursday's event could be acting classes presented by a local amateur theater group. Use your imagination and find out what your customers want to do. Organize horseshoe contests, dance lessons, and special group trips to museums. You will be at the center of all of these much-needed services.

To set up this business, you would rent a small retail space in a shopping center with a lot of pedestrian traffic, preferably located near a retirement home, adult day-care center, senior-citizen center, and churches or synagogues. Your store can be small, perhaps approximately one thousand square feet; expect to pay about $1,000 per month for such a space. You'll need freestanding or wall-mounted racks to hold pamphlets, booklets, forms, and other information that you've collected for your customers. You should have a desk, a table and chairs, and a personal computer (to maintain lists of your customers and participating merchants, create fliers, and maintain your books) with printer.

Make sure you formalize your relationships with participating merchants who are interested in the seniors' business by using a contract drafted by your attorney. Your attorney should also be able to advise you about specific licenses required and recommend the kinds of insurance you'll need. Once your business begins to take off, you may need a part-time employee to assist you by handling your store traffic while you're out; why not select from your growing customer base?

If you received a 10 percent referral fee from one thousand transactions per month at an average transactional cost of $50 each, you would earn $5,000 per month. In addition you would charge your customers a fee to help them fill out the various governmental applications. To ensure that the merchant referral plan works, you should issue a membership card each month to each of your customers. (Refer to Chapter 29, "Cooperative Purchasing," for a similar membership card arrangement.) Only issue the new membership card upon receipt of last month's membership card. Have boxes printed on the back of the card for merchants to mark with their imprint, the merchant's initials, and the gross dollar purchase amount. To encourage use of the card and merchant honesty, and to give you the ability to monitor usage, give prizes to the customers who have spent the most at participating stores. This is the best system to achieve good profit goals and encourage sound business practices.

You may want to consider contacting a local hospital to have them provide a basic health library catering to the group. Transportation companies, hotels, and restaurants would love to give large groups (of any age) discounts to encourage patronage. Although many of these services are available through local senior-citizen clubs, few if any offer the comprehensive, organized services that I envision you offering. What you are doing is providing economic benefits while meeting the social needs of your clients to create a comprehensive business opportunity. A natural progression would be providing services to newcomers to the city or area. Use your imagination and prosper!

You may also want to start a service credit bureau as an ancillary benefit. Members of the bureau who have spare time and are healthy help other members who are ill. For each hour of service they render, they receive a one-hour credit. When the person who has earned service credit hours becomes ill, he or she can call you to arrange for assistance from an able-bodied senior citizen. Whenever service hours are used, you charge the member a $2 per hour management fee. If senior citizens need someone to shop for them, iron clothes, drive them to the doctor's office, cut the grass, shovel the snow, read or write letters, they call your service credit bureau. This would be a wonderful service for all of your members and would virtually guarantee your longevity in business.

For every one hundred hours requested, you earn $200. Of course, you will use your computer to keep track of who has earned what and who owes what. However, I can envision thousands of hours and hundreds of members utilizing this service, so your computer investment will be returned in short order. Before you begin, discuss the concept in detail with your attorney to make sure of your position in regard to state and local employment regulations.

RESOURCES

Association of Retail Marketing Services
Three Caro Ct.
Red Bank, NJ 07701
(201) 842-5070

The Center for Social Gerontology
117 N. First St., Ste. 204
Ann Arbor, MI 48104
(313) 665-1126

Senior Citizens Advocate
40 W. 68th St.
New York, NY 10023
(212) 724-3200

RETAIL STORE FOR SENIOR CITIZENS
LAUNCH CHECKLIST

☐ Meet with your attorney to have merchant agreement drafted. Consider forming a corporation.

☐ Open a bank account.

☐ Obtain IRS tax identification number from your local IRS office.

☐ Order business cards, stationery, and brochure.

☐ Check with your city's business office to determine licensure requirements.

☐ File DBA if appropriate.

☐ Contact a local hospital to determine their interest in participating in your program.

☐ Check with the state unemployment office about jobs for seniors.

☐ Contact governmental agencies for information about housing, income, and medical subsidies.

☐ Contact your insurance agent about business insurance.

☐ Visit local shopping malls and select store location. Have your attorney review the lease before you sign it.

☐ Check with local vocational schools and universities about job-training programs in your community.

☐ Contact transportation companies, hotels, and restaurants to arrange for member discounts.

☐ Purchase a computer for keeping records of member purchases and the service credit bureau activities.

☐ Call on merchants in your community for program participation.

☐ Have membership cards printed.

☐ Write a business plan. Incorporate the knowledge gained from work accomplished on your checklist.

33

Corporate Apartment Rental

We live in a transient society. According to Employee Relocation Council statistics, an estimated half million employees are transferred annually at a cost of about $20 billion. In addition, a corporation often will send a manager to another office temporarily for from one week to six months. It is difficult and stressful for a corporate executive to relocate to a new area and deal with finding a place to live, starting a new job, getting a new driver's license, having utilities turned on in his or her name, and the like. Transfers usually stay in a hotel for a period of time until they get their bearings. The average hotel room today costs a minimum of $150 per day; in New York and Los Angeles, $200 per day won't buy you a very spectacular room. At those rates, that's a whopping $6,000 per month *for the room alone.*

Where there is a need, there is a business opportunity. For a fixed monthly fee, provide these incoming executives with a clean, stylish, well-located, furnished apartment with utilities already turned on, phone already installed, and, if needed, weekly maid service. In addition, you could offer a half-day familiarization tour of the city for a nominal fee. You could introduce the new executive to a reliable real estate agent, a hair salon, dry cleaners, grocery store, and pharmacy, and make other key referrals as requested.

The average apartment landlord deals with a fixed vacancy factor. At any point in the year, the landlord will have a number of units empty, the number varying depending upon the total number of units in the building. The National Apartment Association (NAA) estimates that there are about thirty-five million rental units in the United States. According to the California Apartment Association, the average vacancy factor in California is

4.5 percent, while the national average is 7.4 percent according to the NAA. So if an apartment complex has one hundred apartments, the landlord would average about seven empty units per year in Anytown, USA. If those apartments rented for $750 per month, the building owner is losing $5,250 per month, or $63,000 per year for the seven units. That's a lot of lost money and could be the difference between positive and negative cash flow after the landlord pays the mortgage and operating expenses.

Make a deal with the apartment building owner to rent apartments on the owner's behalf. *Do not rent apartments and then try to find corporate tenants.* That's too risky! Using a contract drafted by your attorney, simply enter into an agreement that the landlord will give you two free months' rent for each ten months you have a paying renter in a unit. That comes to a fee of approximately 17 percent of the annual rent. In some areas, you may be able to charge the landlord 20 percent. This is simply a basic guideline. Obviously, the higher the vacancy rate, the better deal you can negotiate. Let the apartment owner do all of the credit checks as usual.

Of course, your agreement with the landlord is based on availability only. If all of his or her units are full at the time you need one, you can't ask the landlord to evict someone to accommodate your client. However, if the landlord has an empty unit that is fixed up, he or she would be contractually obligated to provide your client with a unit. Don't be too concerned about that provision. There are plenty of good apartment complexes with empty units. If at all possible, find a complex with a physical fitness center, Jacuzzi, and sauna. Today's corporate executives are more health-conscious than ever before.

Next, arrange with a furniture rental store to rent furniture to you at 15 percent off their regular rates. They should give you a discount because you will bring them volume business. If your community does not have a good furniture rental store, simply approach a regular furniture store. Pick out an attractive kitchen set, living room ensemble, and bedroom arrangement. Price the furniture as if you were going to purchase it outright . . . then negotiate with the owner of the store to rent the furniture for a specific period of time. Remember that each new tenant is probably an excellent prospect for the furniture store owner, since the tenant will probably need furniture after moving out of the corporate apartment. The furniture store may elect to give the renter a 5 percent allowance toward the purchase of new furniture as an incentive for your client to go to that store if and when he or she is ready to buy.

Returning to the business deal, assume that the three rooms of furniture are worth $5,000 retail. If the store rents it for $350 per month, they'll receive 100 percent of the retail asking price in a little more than fourteen months. After that, it's found money. What a great opportunity for the furniture store owner— sell a lot more furniture at a much higher price *and* bring in new customers. You, of course, will mark up the furniture store owner's monthly fee by 25 percent (in this case by $87.50) per month.

The furniture store should provide pickup and delivery service at a nominal charge to you. If you can't negotiate the delivery service into your deal, pass the one-time delivery charge on to your client. If you suffer from greed, have the store pick up and deliver for free and then charge your client a one-time $100 delivery charge for your time and effort.

Find out from the landlord what the average utility expense is for his or her units. If, for example, it is $150 per month, add 50 percent and charge your client $225 per month. As part of your service, you will have to call the various utility companies in your area and arrange to have the water, gas, and electricity turned on in your name with the bills to be sent to your home or business address. Your client will have to phone the telephone company and provide the phone to make sure the service is in *his or her* name. *You don't want to be responsible for $10,000 worth of calls to London or Istanbul.*

The marketing is relatively easy. Simply have a one-sheet, one-sided, one-color piece of descriptive literature laid out and printed. The literature will show a picture of a beautiful apartment like the one you will be renting (it doesn't have to be the actual one). Add a floor plan of the apartment, list all of the amenities, and describe your services.

Distribute your brochure to personnel managers, human resources managers, and presidents of local corporations. Large medical clinics, hospitals, and governmental agencies are all great prospects. Give lectures about your business at Optimist and Rotary Club meetings. Another approach is to distribute your brochure to real estate agents (the first place a lot of new people in an area go) and give an agent $100 for each referral. Your service will relieve the pressure of finding a permanent place to live right away.

You, the apartment building landlord, and the furniture store owner could advertise in the local newspaper and split the cost three ways. A $300 ad may be a little steep for any one of you, but a $100 investment will be a little easier for each of you to handle. You get new clients, the landlord gets new tenants, and the furniture store owner sells more furniture at a higher price. In a business where everyone wins, success is almost assured.

What can this business mean for your wallet? First of all, you will make a minimum of 17 percent on a single unit rental. In addition to the two months' free rent, you will also earn $200 per month on the other ten months, due to your monthly markup. That equals $1,500 per year using a base rent of $750 per month. That equals $3,900 per year per apartment ($200 per month $\times$ 12 months = $2,400; $2,400 + $1,050 = $3,900). Add to that amount the $87.50 monthly markup for the furniture rental, or $1,050 per year. Your utilities will bring in another $75 markup per month, or $900 per year. Your total: $5,850 *per unit per year, gross profit.* For every ten units you rent, you earn over $58,000 per year.

If you work out of your home and keep your overhead costs down, you will get huge profits. In large metropolitan areas, I don't think fifty to one hundred rentals is unrealistic. That's almost a quarter-million- to a half-million-dollar business per year. A rule of thumb is that a business that nets a quarter of a million dollars per year is worth approximately four times its earnings. In this case, that equals $1 million. That payback would give an investor a 25 percent per year return on investment, which is more than twice what an investor would earn on money deposited in the bank in most areas of the United States.

You can arrange to provide maid service and simply tack on 25 percent to the maid's daily rate. You can provide linens, cookware, radio, TV, all at premium rates, as easily as you arranged the furniture rentals.

If you add the client's costs of $950 for the apartment, $437 for the furniture, and $225 for utilities, the total monthly expense for a turnkey apartment is $1,612. That's a savings of $4,388 per month when compared to a hotel room at $200 per day. The apartment is larger and more comfortable, and clients can cook their own meals.

Don't overlook the fact that if you already own an apartment or condominium, this business could be an attractive alternative to conventional leasing arrangements. *Everybody* wins in this business, including you!

RESOURCES

Apartment Owners and Managers Association of America
65 Cherry Plaza Ave.
Watertown, CT 06795
(203) 274-2589

National Apartment Association
1111 14th St., NW, Ste. 900
Washington, DC 20005
(202) 842-4050

Apartment Management Magazine
30375 Northwestern Hwy.
Farmington Hills, MI 48334
(313) 737-4477

CORPORATE APARTMENT RENTAL BUSINESS LAUNCH CHECKLIST

☐ Form a company.
☐ Open a checking account.
☐ Visit your local IRS office to obtain an IRS tax identification number.
☐ Obtain city business license if required.
☐ Obtain real estate license if required in your state.
☐ Order business cards and stationery. Lay out brochure and have it printed.
☐ File a DBA if appropriate.

☐ Meet with attorney to draft two apartment rental agreements (one with the building manager and one for the tenant). Also draft a basic agreement for the furniture store.

☐ Arrange for answering service or buy an answering machine.

☐ Obtain appropriate business insurance.

☐ Distribute your brochure and offer to speak to local business associations and club meetings.

☐ Obtain list of real estate agents, companies, hospitals, and governmental agencies in your community.

☐ Contact maid service companies to arrange for discounted services.

☐ Write a business plan. Incorporate the knowledge gained from work accomplished on your checklist.

34

New-Business Development Center

It's estimated that over one million enterprises are opening their doors every year in the United States. Whether a new retail store, personal service business, manufacturing company, hotel, hospital, funeral home, or construction company, each has unique characteristics and corresponding needs. Small Business Administration data show that twenty-four of every one hundred businesses opening their doors today will have gone out of business in two years; twenty-seven more will have disappeared in two more years.

Thinking before launching a specific business is obviously critical to its success, and there are countless details that have to be taken care of. Although every business is different, each has common, similar kinds of needs at start-up. I discussed starting your own business brokerage company—the business of selling businesses—in Chapter 16. New-business development is helping people establish a business.

Did you know that anyone can call Prentice-Hall Corporate Services (part of Simon & Schuster) and hire the firm to form a corporation anywhere in the United States for less than $500 in most cases? They have locations in Atlanta, Boston, Chicago, Dallas, Houston, Los Angeles, New York City, Philadelphia, San Francisco, Washington, D.C., Trenton, New Jersey, and Dover, Delaware. For a nominal charge, Prentice-Hall can also register your company in any state in which you want to do business. Their corporate specialists can assist you with document preparation and filing, representation services, and other specialized services. A person can save approximately $1,000 by simply having access to this resource, since an attorney would easily charge $1,500 to provide the same service.

Every new company that is not a sole proprietorship needs to obtain a tax identification number from the Internal Revenue Service. A new business may need to obtain a business license, publish a fictitious business name (DBA statement), or apply for a resale tax permit. Many new businesses need health permits, liquor licenses, and special governmental authorizations. In a new-business development center, for a fee, *you* provide these services.

New retail store owners need advice on location opportunities. Visit the city traffic department and obtain counts of vehicular traffic for certain streets in your community. You could pick up chamber of commerce literature and hand it out to business-people moving into the area. Retail store owners will need help understanding leases. Perhaps you could afford the one-time cost of having an attorney review two or three standard leases and have the attorney mark them up with recommended changes for the benefit of the tenant. For specific questions related to legal issues, your customers could be referred to a legal specialist.

Contact banks in your area and obtain new-account applications, loan applications, and merchant credit card programs. Obtain application forms for computerized payroll services and printed information on other new-business services offered to people starting businesses in the community.

You should have information on corporate auto-leasing programs and on leasing equipment including computers, telephone systems, and office furniture. You should have applications for Federal Express and UPS accounts, as well as corporate credit cards. You may want to have a list of attorneys, accountants, and business consultants in the area. Check with the attorney referral service in your area for names of attorneys who specialize in business law. Interview a few accountants and ascertain their enthusiasm to develop relationships with new businesses. Meet with business consultants in your area and determine their capabilities by verifying references and checking with your local Better Business Bureau.

Basically you are doing the legwork for your customer. These are just a few of the myriad of tasks the new-business owner has to contend with when starting a business. He or she also needs to fill out credit applications and order business cards, stationery, accounting ledgers, and office supplies.

Marketing your business is relatively easy. Simply read your local newspaper for new DBA listings. Check with the office of the secretary of state in your state capital for corporation applications. Every time a new business contacts one of your referral sources, that business should tell the prospect about your service. You will probably have at least fifty attorneys, accountants, leasing companies, office furniture stores, consultants, auto dealerships, and printers recommending you. They will recommend you because they know that you have new-business customers from all of these *other* referral sources who could be referred *back* to them by you.

So how do you make money? You charge a 10 percent referral fee to each merchant used by your customer. Your customer pays you an initial consultation fee of $50 plus a fee for each service required. In other words, if your customer wants you to get his IRS tax identification number, you charge an initial fee of $50 and then $15 to $30 for that particular service. A fee chart would look similar to the following illustration:

Service	Fee
Initial consultation (includes business referrals)	$50
IRS tax identification number	25
Sales tax permit (+ cash deposit)	25
DBA listing (+ newspaper listing cost)	25
Retail store traffic analysis	235
Comparative rent rate analysis	45
Health permit application (+ license fee)	90
City business license application (+ license fee)	35
SBA loan assistance	65

A very important concern for someone who has a new business or one with fewer than fifteen employees is the high cost of hospitalization insurance. Investors in a new business venture and banks lending money to a new business may want the owners to buy key-employee insurance; in case the business owner dies, the investor and/or banker could use the life insurance proceeds to operate the business while a new manager is being found. Several insurance agencies specialize in insurance packages for new businesses. After interviewing your customers to determine their needs, you can assist them by recommending which insurance firms offer the best protection for each category of insurance at the best price.

Over a six-month period, I think you are going to be amazed with the response. Design and print a basic one-page brochure that outlines your services and rates. Place these brochures on the counters of your participating retail merchants. Educate accountants, attorneys, and business consultants to instruct their clients who are starting a new business to call you.

Initially, you can work out of your home and set up appointments at each potential customer's facility. Eventually, as business picks up, you will want to consider setting up a small retail store next door to or at least near a major stationery or photocopying store. Most new businesses have office supply and photocopying needs, and you'll want to catch the owners early in the game as they set up their new business.

Every new-business owner should be given an introduction card filled out by you to tell each participating merchant that the new business is a commissionable sale to you. (This concept is similar to that mentioned in Chapters 29, "Cooperative Purchasing," and 32, "Retail Store for Senior Citizens.") Keep a record of each referral, so that you can track your revenues and periodically verify sales by calling your customers.

RESOURCES

American Management Association
135 W. 50th St.
New York, NY 10020
(212) 586-8100

Business Professional Association
100 Metroplex Dr.
Edison, NJ 08817
(201) 985-4441

Business Forms and Systems Magazine
401 N. Broad St.
Philadelphia, PA 19108
(215) 238-5300

Entrepreneur Magazine
2392 Morse Ave.
Irvine, CA 92714
(714) 261-2325

Venture Magazine
521 Fifth Ave.
New York, NY 10175
(212) 682-7373

How to Write a Winning Business Plan
by Joseph Mancuso
Simon and Schuster

NEW-BUSINESS DEVELOPMENT CENTER
LAUNCH CHECKLIST

☐ Form a corporation.
☐ Open a bank account.
☐ Obtain IRS tax identification number from IRS office.
☐ Order business cards, stationery, and brochures.
☐ Obtain required business licenses from your city business office.
☐ Investigate insurance coverage needs.
☐ Investigate office location possibilities.
☐ Contact chamber of commerce for local demographic information.
☐ Contact city traffic department for information about vehicular traffic.

☐ Contact local banks for various applications.

☐ Check with attorney referral service.

☐ Contact auto leasing, computer leasing, telephone, and office furniture companies for their applications and referral fees where applicable.

☐ Check with the secretary of state's office in your state for new corporate applications.

☐ Establish working relationship with accountants, attorneys, auto dealers, printers, and other key suppliers to new businesses.

☐ Place a yellow pages advertisement.

☐ Distribute your brochure.

☐ Contact all city, county, state, and federal regulatory agencies to obtain appropriate filing documents.

☐ Write a business plan. Incorporate the knowledge gained from work accomplished on your checklist.

35

Valet Parking Service

How many restaurants have you visited that don't have valet parking? I have traveled extensively all over the United States and Canada. Much to my surprise, many fine restaurants don't have valet parking. I always use the convenient valet service because it saves time and I like the good feeling that someone is keeping an eye on my car. I remember paying a young man in Rome, Italy, to keep an eye on my rented Mercedes, only to find him stealing my radio. But that was Italy and he was a street-smart thief. Thank goodness that I have a sense of humor! If I had not paid him, he probably would have stolen the entire car! In some metropolitan areas, the car may be parked on the street, locked, and unattended. The only advantage in this instance is the convenience of front-door service. On a cold night that could be a big consideration.

Prospecting is very easy. Simply drive around town several evenings and identify nice restaurants without valet parking service. Restaurant managers are usually busy during the lunch and dinner hours, so you'll probably want to discuss your proposal with them between 10:00 A.M. and noon or between 2:00 P.M. and 5:00 P.M.

The business proposition is easy. With the agreement that you and your attorney have written in hand, tell the restaurateur that for every customer's car you park, you will charge the customer $1.50 and give the restaurant owner $.50. (Some valet parking services pay the restaurant a flat monthly fee. What you charge your customers will vary depending upon your agreement with the restaurant and your location. Find out what other valet parking services charge for comparable restaurant locations and similar clientele.)

Just imagine—the owner actually makes additional revenue by providing a wonderful service to customers that doesn't cost him or her a penny! That's a pragmatic business opportunity that should appeal to every restaurateur you talk to. By charging $1.50, you can expect that almost everyone will give you $2.00. Thus, you will, in fact, keep $1.50 for each car parked. Although actual numbers will vary by restaurant, if you park just forty cars per weeknight and one hundred cars per weekend night, for a mere investment of four to five hours of your time each evening, you could earn over $600 per week.

This service business is easy to market, easy to sell, doesn't require any specialized training, and doesn't require a large cash layout. What does it require? A key box—homemade if you're handy, since a commercial hardwood key box holding about fifty keys costs $70 to $80, and an iron box would cost between $200 and $300. You may want to invest in a red vest embroidered with your company name for under $50. If you don't want to spend the additional money initially, wear a white shirt and black slacks. A bow tie always looks good. If start-up capital is not a problem, Valet Park International (2052 Highway 35, Ste. 204, Wall Township, NJ 07719; [908] 974-0677 or [800] PARK-123) offers the only valet parking franchise in the United States for approximately $39,900.

The restaurant's general liability policy may cover your insurance needs, but often the parking service must take care of its own insurance needs as well as the maintenance of the restaurant's parking lot, so confer with your attorney about your responsibilities. Each car owner will probably have collision and comprehensive insurance. Make sure your claim check indemnifies you from all liability while the customer's car is parked. Preprinted, two- or three-part parking tickets with standard liability contract language can be purchased from local printers for about $10 per thousand. Check with the experts to make sure the standard language provides you with enough protection. Typically, the liability disclaimers discourage lawsuits but seldom hold up in a court of law.

Depending upon the location of the restaurant and whether or not the restaurant has its own lot, you may find that you have to rent parking space in order to handle the number of cars anticipated. Frequently, downtown parking lots are busy during the day, but they may be in need of customers at night, so you may be able to negotiate a very good deal for parking there during the evening hours. Gas stations are another possibility for additional parking. If possible, pass any additional charges on to your customers. For example, if your negotiated parking lot fee averages out to $1.00 for each car that you expect to park, your rate would go up to $2.50. Since in most cases you'll receive $3.00 from each customer, you'll keep $2.50 and be able to pay the restaurant without dipping into your profits.

Consider offering your valet service to local shopping centers. Such a service is especially popular during hectic holiday seasons. In selected locations in San Francisco and Los Angeles, upscale department stores and malls offer valet parking for their shoppers. What a great merchandising plan! Shopping malls all over the country should be similarly interested in contracting for valet parking.

Chuck Pick, "car parker to the stars," got a job at age sixteen parking cars at Romanoff's in Los Angeles. Now owner of his own parking service, he remembers one disastrous night at Chasen's restaurant in Beverly Hills when someone knocked over the pegboard holding over two hundred sets of keys—perhaps one hundred of which were Mercedes keys, which all look alike! Today, Chuck's company handles approximately twelve hundred events per year. With hard work, persistence, and a pleasant, outgoing personality, you, too, could develop a very lucrative business.

RESOURCES

National Parking Association
1112 16th St., NW, Ste. 300
Washington, DC 20036
(202) 296-4336

Parking Magazine
1112 16th St., NW, Ste. 300
Washington, DC 20036
(202) 296-4336

VALET PARKING SERVICE LAUNCH CHECKLIST

☐ Form a corporation.
☐ Have attorney review restaurant agreement and parking ticket language.
☐ Open a bank account.
☐ Obtain city business license if required.
☐ Order business cards and stationery.
☐ Obtain IRS tax identification number.
☐ Order claim checks.
☐ Obtain required insurance coverage.
☐ Build or purchase a key board.
☐ Contact restaurants, hospitals, and shopping malls to determine their level of interest.
☐ Write a business plan. Incorporate the knowledge gained from work accomplished on your checklist.

36

Dating Service

Millions of dollars are spent every year in the United States for matchmaking services. Almost 40 percent of the female population in the United States and almost 35 percent of the male population is either single, divorced, or widowed. Most people don't want to sit in bars and lounges and wait for Mr. or Ms. Right to come along. Many people are lonely and isolated and aren't sure where to go to find companionship. But life is hectic, and people often don't have time or make time to attend to their most important need of all—love!

Wherever there is a need, there is an opportunity. Consider mail-order matchmaking. All you need to start is a personal computer and a camera. Start by finding out how many dating services already exist in your community. What services do they offer? Do they specialize? Next, check with the Census Bureau to make sure there are enough singles in your area to support your business. Once you're satisfied that there is a market for your service, proceed to design a questionnaire and ask each aspiring candidate for some personal information, such as age, sex, educational background, marital status, height, weight, color of eyes and hair, etc. Then inquire about each person's ideal mate's requirements, such as physical attributes, educational background, social bearing, sports, hobbies, and leisure activities. Then photograph each customer in several poses.

Open a file on each customer and input all of this data into your computer, then begin matching up needs and desires with your on-line inventory of candidates. Initially you can do visual comparisons. Eventually, as your business grows, you will compare your clients' requirements against inventory automatically with your computer.

Charge between $150 and $1,000 per match, depending on the scope of your program. Each of your customers should sign a contract drafted by your attorney outlining your services and policies. One woman in Denver is making over $13,000 per month at home using her personal computer *after only twelve months in business.*

Your marketing program can be as inexpensive as one-page flyers placed under windshield-wiper blades on cars parked in apartment and condominium complexes, Laundromats, and movie theater parking lots. Or you can assemble a four-color brochure that depicts the joys of having a close, loving relationship, with photographs of happy couples sharing their lives together. One thing to keep in mind: if you're successful in this business, you will *lose* your customers!

In an effort to protect your clients from unscrupulous characters, run credit checks and/or criminal checks as a service. You can purchase these investigation checks for a nominal fee by contacting a company like Information Resource Service Company (3777 N. Harbor Blvd., Fullerton, CA 92635: [714] 526-8485). The cost for this service is a corporate membership of $250 plus a $30 monthly maintenance fee and the charges for any searches they conduct. Provide a wonderful service for people who may never meet the right person any other way.

Eventually, you may want to enlarge the scope of your business. Singles groups such as ski clubs, dance groups, or Parents Without Partners may be in need of a newsletter service, which you can provide for a fee. You may decide to specialize. Today there is a growing number of singles services catering to a particular niche, such as the safe-sex singles groups that provide "romance without risk" or advanced-degree clubs whose members are required to have at least a master's degree to participate. You could create a search service exclusively for business executives and collect substantial fees by providing your clients with potential spousal candidates.

For fees beginning at $5,000, Christine O'Keefe of Beverly Hills, California, will spend time screening potential mates and introduce each client to up to twelve candidates. Clients also are screened; only 10 percent of the twenty-five hundred applicants per year are accepted by Ms. O'Keefe. She states that approximately 60 percent of her clients find a serious relationship as a result of her services. Who knows, if you are single, you might even find the right mate yourself while running your own business.

DATING SERVICE LAUNCH CHECKLIST

- ☐ Form a company.
- ☐ Open a bank account.
- ☐ Order business cards, stationery, and brochures.
- ☐ Obtain IRS tax identification number from local IRS office.
- ☐ File DBA with local newspaper if you elect to use a sole proprietorship or partnership instead of a corporation.
- ☐ Obtain city business license if required.
- ☐ Purchase a personal computer, word-processing and database package, printer, and camera if you do not already have these items.
- ☐ Have attorney draft client contract.
- ☐ Distribute brochures to apartment complexes and Laundromats, and place them on parked automobiles.
- ☐ Open an office in your home or nearby office building. Since many customers will be visiting your office, weigh the convenience and cost-effectiveness of a home office against your need for privacy.
- ☐ Write a business plan. Incorporate the knowledge gained from work accomplished on your checklist.

37

Tire Removal and Disposal Service

Did you ever wonder what happens to your old tire after it's replaced with a new one? Jack Zimmer, an analyst with Goodyear Tire and Rubber Company, reports that about 250 million tires are discarded in the United States each year. Since some tire discards are large truck tires, this number is the equivalent of between 300 and 350 million passenger tires (*The Conservationist*, February–March 1990). The stockpile in the United States alone is estimated at over three billion tires, according to the *Economist* (August 11, 1990). Only about 30 percent of these discarded tires are ever used productively, and only 10 percent are landfilled properly. Approximately 60 percent are disposed of illegally (*American City & County*, May 1990). At least twenty states now have waste tire laws or regulations. For instance, in New York, all facilities with more than one thousand tires must recycle 75 percent or more of the tires accumulated each year. Landfills may charge up to $5 per tire or $30 to $35 per ton for tire discards.

No one seems to know what to do with discarded tires, but tires continue to be manufactured by the billions. One inventive young man shipped ten tons of old used tires by train from St. Louis to Boston C.O.D. The party in Boston never claimed the shipment, since there was no person to receive them in the first place. It was simply a way to unload ten tons of tires.

Another creative man leased 160 acres from a farmer near Sacramento, California. After he told the farmer he needed the land to grow corn, he paid the first month's rent. After forty-five days, the farmer drove out to the property to find out why he had not received the rent for the second month. Instead of his tenant and a field of newly sown corn, he found a mountain of old discarded tires. Guess what? The man was nowhere to be found.

With environmental concerns increasingly on the minds of Americans, you could turn an environmental problem into a profitable business. Retail stores and gas stations will actually pay you to pick up old tires and dispose of them. Of course, since the railroads probably won't fall for the old one-way-to-Boston-C.O.D. routine, the first problem is to find a legal way to discard the tires. Although tires make up only 1 percent of the solid wastes, they are extraordinarily difficult to deal with, since they rise to the tops of landfills the way zombies rise from graves in movies. They are also highly flammable and often shelter rodents and mosquitoes. Shredded tires are less likely to burn and pose less of an environmental hazard, but shredding requires special equipment. Tires cannot be burned in the usual manner because the resultant toxic smoke contains chemicals known to cause leukemia and kidney and liver damage. Also, since petroleum is a major component of every tire, tire fires are almost impossible to put out. In 1984, a fire in Catskill, New York, burned an estimated four to six million tires. It took hundreds of fire fighters over one week to control the surface burning alone; it was months, however, before the below-the-surface fire, caused by the oil released during the burning of the tires' exteriors, burned out.

Believe it or not, there are a couple of solutions to the tire disposal problem other than selling them for backyard swings. Recycling may take the form of retreading, but unfortunately consumers are generally not attracted to retreads when they can buy a new tire for almost the same price. Luckily, the number of retreaded truck tires has stayed fairly constant. Used tires may also be used as dock bumpers and railroad ties. Tires have also been used in constructing underwater reefs to enhance fishing opportunities.

Another option that could potentially use great amounts of tires is shredding. If shredded finely enough, tires may be used in carpet underlays, car and walkway mats, sports surfaces, and road repairs. The reuse of tires as rubber crumbs in asphalt pavement has been increasing at a rate of 30 percent per year (*Modern Tire Dealer*, Mid-April 1990).

Many believe that the most economical and potentially most

lucrative way of solving the problem is to use tires for fuel in waste-to-energy plants. Pound per pound, tires hold more energy than high-quality coal. Today there are at least twenty industrial facilities using tires as a fuel source. Since there are probably enough tires sitting in junkyards, dump sites, and storage sites to go to the moon if stacked on top of each other, this could be a profitable business if you're resourceful and willing to work hard.

First, check state and local regulations to see if there are any tire storage prohibitions. Then rent a storage site, preferably outside city limits, making sure that you inform the owner of the site of your intentions and that you are in compliance with any storage restrictions. Contact all of your potential sources of old tires and tell each that you will charge a removal fee of fifty to seventy-five cents per tire. Run as many trailer loads as you can to your storage site.

Next check with your potential *buying* sources. You could sell to dock manufacturers and installers, since tires are perfect for a variety of needs in marinas. Contact state highway departments, which could use the tires in building and resurfacing roads. They may also be used at the end of steep grades to stop runaway trucks. Don't forget building contractors, shredding facilities, and waste-to-energy plants either. If you can get your buyers to pay the freight to their location site, you will have created a great business opportunity from a great problem. If you can load an average of one thousand tires per day, at fifty cents each, you will earn $500 per day or $10,000 per month less the trailer rental fee, gasoline charges, and storage site rent. Eventually you can buy your own trailer or truck from your profits.

Norm Emanuel, owner of Emanuel Tire Company in Baltimore and the "guru of tire recycling," has been recycling discarded tires since 1957 and shredding them since 1979. Considered one of the few people who is seriously tackling the problem, he is making money while disposing of tires on a large scale. Norm's success story is representative of his belief that only through free enterprise and by allowing people to make a profit can communities with scrap tire problems be cleaned up, reports *Modern Tire Dealer* (Mid-April 1990). Annually he disposes of approximately four million tires he receives from his large sources in five states and the District of Columbia and from some thirty smaller-scale collectors who buy tires from service stations and individuals. Norm even disposes of Baltimore's city and school district tires free of charge. He believes he is the reason that you won't find discarded tires anywhere in Baltimore.

The problem of tire disposal exists all over the world. Once you solidify your buying sources, the potential is there for you to franchise the idea almost anywhere and make some serious money!

RESOURCES

American Retreaders' Association
P.O. Box 17203
Louisville, KY 40217
(502) 367-9133

National Recycling Coalition
1101 30th St., NW, #305
Washington, DC 20007
(202) 625-6406

National Tire Dealers and Retreaders Association
1250 I St., NW, Ste. 400
Washington, DC 20005
(800) 87-NTDRA

Tire Retread Information Bureau
26555 Carmel Ranch Blvd., Ste. 3
Carmel, CA 93923
(408) 625-3247

Modern Tire Dealer
Bill Communications, Inc.
341 White Pond Dr.
P.O. Box 8391
Akron, OH 44320
(216) 867-4401

Tire Business
Crain Communications Inc.
1725 Merriman Rd., #300
Akron, OH 44313-5251
(216) 836-9180

TIRE REMOVAL AND DISPOSAL SERVICE
LAUNCH CHECKLIST

☐ Form a corporation.
☐ Open a checking account.
☐ Obtain city business license if required.
☐ Purchase business cards and stationery.
☐ Have attorney check city, county, and state laws relative to the storage of tires and research any restrictions that may affect you.
☐ Select storage site and negotiate lease. Have attorney review the lease.
☐ Obtain IRS tax identification number.
☐ Rent trailer and have hitch attached to your automobile or arrange for the use of a truck.
☐ Have attorney draft tire removal contract for your sources to sign.
☐ Sell your service to tire stores and other sources of scrap tires.
☐ Locate alternative sources for tire disposal.
☐ Write a business plan. Incorporate the knowledge gained from work accomplished on your checklist.

38

Health Walking

Americans are more health-conscious today than ever before. They are watching their cholesterol levels and blood pressure and controlling what is in their diet. Smoking in public places is becoming increasingly difficult. Thanks to a tremendous public health awareness campaign launched by the makers of Fleischmann's margarine, Quaker Oats cereal, Nike athletic shoes, and other products, Americans are exercising like never before. Health clubs, fitness centers, and diet centers are prospering.

Many consumers are looking for a comfortable, safe, and enjoyable place to exercise without the expense of joining a health club. Frequently people cannot or will not run, jog, or walk in cold or rainy weather, and others, especially women and elderly people, are afraid to exercise outdoors in their own neighborhoods because they consider them dangerous.

What better place than the neighborhood shopping mall to get the exercise they need? According to *American Demographics* (April 1990), the typical American regional shopping center is an enclosed mall containing at least 400,000 square feet of selling space. The lengthy runways, flat floors, constant temperature, quiet atmosphere, built-in security, and lack of polluted air and traffic make it an attractive exercise environment. Plus, there are approximately three thousand possible sites available. According to the Roper Organization, shoppers' enjoyment of browsing has diminished since 1985, and because profits are shrinking in much of the shopping center industry, the centers are looking for ways to increase customer traffic. The subliminal effects of mall walking could obviously be beneficial to merchants; one mall jogger in Paramus, New Jersey, confessed to spending over $400 on shoes in one month!

Shopping malls usually open around 9:00 A.M. or 10:00 A.M. and close between 6:00 P.M. and 9:00 P.M. daily. With the approval of the shopping mall manager, arrange for daily walks from 7:00 A.M. to 9:00 A.M. The 7:00 A.M. to 7:30 A.M. group could be a beginners group, walking more slowly than the 7:30 A.M. to 8:00 A.M. class. The last two half-hour walking groups would walk more strenuously, really working up a sweat. Each participant would be allowed to use the mall free of charge.

Women selected fitness walking their most popular sport in 1989, reports *Women's Sports and Fitness* magazine (September 1990), with approximately twice the number of participants (40.6 million) as in each of the runner-up sports of swimming, aerobics, and cycling. Avia footwear estimates that there may be as many as 500,000 mall walkers in the United States. To attract some of these walkers to your mall, post your one-page flyer on bulletin boards of senior-citizen clubs, fitness centers, churches, hospitals, universities, and bowling alleys and near the cashier at retail stores and restaurants.

How do you make money? Remember, I said certain advertisers want to reach groups of health-conscious people. Contact health food stores in your area, sports clothing stores, health magazines, sports medicine physicians, chiropractors, and fitness centers, and sell them a response card participation program for $250 per month each. Print one thousand index cards containing an advertisement for the store for each participating merchant. Distribute the cards to the mall walkers and ask them whenever they patronize the respective stores to tell each sponsoring merchant that they learned about the store as a result of participating in your mall walkers group.

Sell T-shirts as well as books on walking and exercise from a small folding table you set up each morning in the mall. You will want to issue certificates of accomplishment or award medals to participants who complete one hundred miles, five hundred miles, and one thousand miles, for example. In addition to awarding medals, the Grossmont Center Mall Walking Club of San Diego County publishes the walking milestones of its thirteen thousand members in a newsletter.

Mall walkers are typically mature buyers who have the spending power for "after-exercise shopping," since the fifty-plus age group (over 63 million adults) controls at least 50 percent of the country's discretionary income. According to Donnelley Marketing's 1989 study of the mature market, five characteristics are selling points to mature customers that shopping mall owners and merchants could capitalize upon with mall walkers: security, quality, comfort and convenience, socialization, and recognition. Because mall walking goes hand in hand with window shopping, merchants in the mall may want to seize upon this opportunity by advertising the walks in their store displays and media ads, by participating in the awards programs, and by giving merchandise discounts to walkers who earn certificates.

One mall walkers company in Florida has an average of sixty participating merchants. At $250 each per month, that equates to $15,000 per month, and, of course, the business can be expanded to nearby towns. The merchants pay their sponsoring fees in advance, so you won't have to advance the advertising card money.

The mall walkers will love the social aspects of meeting and exercising on a regular basis. According to a story in the *Saturday Evening Post* (September 1989), Mary Paladino, sixty, met her husband Jim, seventy-five, while mall walking. Five months later, the two tied the knot at the shopping center, holding the ceremony at 9:00 A.M. so that any guests who wanted to could exercise first! Three of the mall's fast-food shops catered the affair, and other mall shops provided the wedding cake, tuxedos, invitations, flowers, and music. As a result of the wedding, Avia sent the celebrity mall walkers around the country to promote a new walking shoe designed "to give extra traction for smoother, slicker mall floors."

RESOURCES

Walking Association
P.O. Box 37228
Tucson, AZ 85704
(602) 742-9589

The Walking Magazine
9–11 Harcourt St.
Boston, MA 02116
(617) 266-3322

HEALTH WALKING BUSINESS LAUNCH CHECKLIST

☐ Form a corporation.

☐ Open a bank account.

☐ Obtain an IRS tax identification number from IRS office.

☐ Order business cards, stationery, and brochures from a local printer.

☐ Obtain city business license if required.

☐ Contact shopping mall managers to discuss mall participation and related activities. Select one mall for your business.

☐ Contact your attorney about drafting an agreement between your company and the mall. Ask the mall management for a copy of its insurance policies. Ask to be indemnified from all liability.

☐ Obtain resale tax permit if you intend to sell T-shirts, books, and other related items.

☐ Visit with mall merchants to sell them on participation.

☐ Distribute your brochures.

☐ Contact advertising participants.

☐ Write a business plan. Incorporate the knowledge gained from work accomplished on your checklist.

39

Pet-Grooming Service

Packard Facts Inc., a New York–based market research firm, estimates that $2.3 billion was spent on pet care and related accessories in 1989. People love their pets, and they especially love clean pets! Most pet owners hate washing their pets, and if they don't mind, few have the time. You may launch a mobile cleaning business and later expand into other areas of pet care, such as providing insurance or burial services. T. Keith Grove of Vero Beach, Florida, is one of the only seventeen American pet dentists. A periodontist in the morning, he works on cats and dogs in the afternoon. His fees range from $150 to $800, and he'll even perform doggie orthodontist work!

Local pet stores often offer a pet-cleaning service. For approximately $25 they'll wash your dog, fluff it dry, spray on a little canine cologne, and wait for you to pick it up. For fees up to $50, some offer a deluxe grooming service that may include a flea bath, nail trim, coat treatment, and designer cut. In Manhattan and Beverly Hills, you can probably double these cost estimates. Bev Dennison, who began as a hairdresser, created a pampered pet salon where animals are groomed, exercised, and given play periods and cookie breaks. Linda Coffey of Minneapolis introduced Haute Canine dog treats in the early eighties and now sells about sixty items, including $3 "treating cards" for pets. In *Success* magazine (October 1990), she reported that sales hit the $1 million mark in 1989. Once you establish a good customer base with your pet-grooming service, you may want to add other profit-producing opportunities.

The marketing part of the mobile cleaning service for pets is relatively easy. Make the local veterinarians your partners by giving them $3 for each referral. Research what other grooming services are charging, and charge customers the same price they'd pay at local pet stores. Remember: you are going to them. This saves each customer travel time while eliminating the inconvenience and potential of pet "accidents" in the family sedan. Prepare a simple, one-page brochure describing your services and include a complete fee schedule. These should be left on the counters at all participating vets' offices and could also be placed near the cashier at any pet stores that do not offer grooming services.

You will need a large, sturdy tub, a pair of battery-operated shears for trimming, hair clippers, nail clippers, dog brushes, flea combs, two leashes, a "loop" or noose to hold the pet's head, regular and flea shampoo, a hair dryer, a pair of heavy-duty rubber gloves, a strong table, a hose, and, of course, dog biscuits to reward the pets.

All of these may be purchased from your local pet store and hardware store. Purchase equipment directly from the manufacturer whenever possible, and buy used equipment if it's available. The pet store clerk may have to order the battery-operated shears, since they may not be stocked. You should be able to get all of these items for under $200.

If you lack experience, volunteer to work at a local grooming service to get the hands-on training you require. There are, of course, occupational hazards: dogs bite and cats scratch. Owners will be certain that you somehow provoked the attack. "Fufu never bit anyone before," they will say. Wear gloves and be careful when handling dogs. Your local veterinarian can give you some tips on how to minimize the risks of handling animals. You will at some time, no doubt, clip a dog too closely or nick an ear. Have your vet recommend a good, basic antiseptic for such occasions. Check with your attorney about what liability insurance you should carry.

Place all of your equipment in your truck, van, or trunk of your car, and you are in business. Eventually, you will probably want to purchase a van with a sliding side door so that you may install pet-grooming stations where animal movement is restricted during the shearing, trimming, and clipping operations. A used recreational vehicle with showers already built in is another option. I think that you'll discover that carrying your supplies in and out of a vehicle will get pretty tiresome quickly.

There should be no shortage of customers, since the American Veterinary Medical Association estimates there are over 100 million dogs and cats that are household companions. If you wash an average of ten pets per day (many families have multiple pets), you will earn between $250 and $500 per day, plus tips. That equates to $5,000 to $10,000 per month per grooming team. Some grooming services actually deliver pet food and other pet care items at a 10 percent markup over cost.

As a side note, there are several insurance companies that specialize in offering both medical and death benefits for pets. You may want to sell benefits packages to your grooming customers for their pets and increase your profits.

One creative couple in Chattanooga, Tennessee, rents a small city park each year and hosts a dog, cat, and unusual-pet contest. They select local dog trainers as judges. They charge a nominal fee to enter, and the first-place award is a blue ribbon and one year of grooming. (What if a frog wins the unusual-pet contest? How do you groom a frog?)

The opportunities are endless in this growing, dynamic market. If you love animals, this may be the perfect business for you.

RESOURCES

National Dog Groomers Association of America
Box 101
Clark, PA 16113
(412) 962-2711

Pet Industry Joint Advisory Council
1710 Rhode Island Ave., NW
Washington, DC 20036
(202) 452-1525

Professional Association of Pet Industries
2475 San Ramon Valley, #7
San Ramon, CA 94583
(415) 838-0887

Pet Business Magazine
13506 Dallas Lane
Carmel, IN 46032
(317) 571-9007

PET-GROOMING SERVICE LAUNCH CHECKLIST

☐ Consult your attorney about the possibility of forming a limited partnership with veterinarians in your community.

☐ Open a bank account.

☐ Obtain an IRS tax identification number from IRS office.

☐ Order business cards, stationery, and brochures.

☐ Obtain resale tax permit if you intend to sell pet supplies.

☐ File a DBA with your local newspaper.

☐ Obtain a city business license if required.

☐ Contact veterinarians for limited partnership participation and/or referrals.

☐ Obtain required business insurance.

☐ Purchase the required tools and supplies.

☐ Contact insurance companies that offer medical and death benefits for pets.

☐ Place advertisement in yellow pages.

☐ Distribute brochures.

☐ Write a business plan. Incorporate the knowledge gained from work accomplished on your checklist.

40

Employing the Handicapped

U.S. News & World Report (June 4, 1990) states that there are 43.6 million Americans with a wide variety of physical or mental disabilities. The Census Bureau reports that, due to a disability, over 13 million Americans aged sixteen to sixty-four are restricted in the amount or type of work they are able to do. Of that group, only 36 percent of the men and 28 percent of the women are actually in the work force. Twenty percent of the adults who suffer from a work disability have an income below the poverty level.

Although new legislation will make discrimination against the disabled illegal, those who are currently in the work force with full-time, year-round jobs still earn approximately 20 percent less than other employees. Depending upon the disability, travel for the handicapped may be restricted or impossible, making it difficult for them to join the traditional work force. Think of the millions of potentially useful human beings sitting in their homes day after day, feeling useless, hopeless, depressed, and unproductive. This is one of the greatest employment resources in America. Yet the percentage of disabled persons in the work force has declined during the last decade as their actual population has grown.

Have I got a business for you—a business in which everybody wins. Train the handicapped to make a good, above-average living at home. Are you a computer programmer? Word processor? A VCR repairperson? Tutor? Proofreader? Editor? Phone salesperson? Do you possess a skill that you can easily teach to others? Transfer your skills to the handicapped and pay them good wages to increase your business, productivity, and profit margins. The introduction of computer technology into the workplace has made many more jobs dependent upon intellect rather than physical strength or abilities. A good mind is a precious commodity and may only require retraining. Tap into this greatly underutilized employee pool.

A large percentage of semiprecious and precious stones are cut in Taiwan. The Taiwanese craftspeople work inexpensively and fast, which frequently results in abominable quality. The next time you look at a brilliant-cut gem such as a blue topaz stone, ruby, or sapphire, look at the crown (top) and pavilion (the surface that slants outward) to see if the cuts are even. If they are not, it was probably cut in Taiwan. Sometimes gems are cut so fast that precious material is wasted. This kind of workmanship creates poor depth of field, diffraction, shine, and brilliance.

A retired gemologist (expert in semiprecious and precious stones) in Reno, Nevada, cut stones for a hobby. He bought the raw stones wholesale, cut them on his facetting machine, and sold them at a premium because of their great and unusual quality. His next-door neighbor had kidney disease and was bored to death because he was unable to return to his job. The gemologist taught him how to use the facetting machine in three days, provided him with raw gemstones from local jewelers, and his next-door neighbor began facetting stones. He won awards at gemological shows and made more money at home doing something he came to love than he had ever made at his Department of Water and Power job before he became disabled.

Our gemologist friend went on to train twenty-three other handicapped people in the Reno area. As a group they now produce a significant percentage of the cut semiprecious stones sold in California today. Perhaps you like jewelry and would consider taking a class at your local gemological school in facetting stones. A facetting machine costs about $1,400 to $1,500, and your supplies would cost less than $100. You could then teach others to facet stones in their homes.

People in many professions have more work than they can handle. So often we hear people say, "If only I could clone myself, I would be rich." If you own a secretarial service for example, and you have more manuscripts, resumes, and proposals than you know what to do with, why not train the handicapped in word processing? Instead of turning work away or alienating customers by missing deadlines, use this great resource. Many people working out of their homes will already have computers and appropriate software or be familiar with the programs you use. An additional bonus: you won't have to provide office space, parking, or equipment. If you pay a flat fee per page, you will lock in your cost to do business and your profit margin. I know a magazine editor in San Francisco who routinely farms out over 50 percent of his editing to handicapped editors who work out of their homes.

Locate handicapped people by buying subscribers' lists to magazines for the handicapped; contact a mailing list brokerage company for quotes. Usually the costs for mailing lists average about $70 to $100 per thousand names. Advertise in your local newspaper that you are seeking the disabled for job training. There are hospital rehabilitation centers, Veterans Administration placement offices, colleges and university placement offices, and physicians in your community that you should also contact for leads.

Leave fliers or brochures about your proposed program in doctors' offices and hospital administration offices. Attend public meetings for the handicapped so that you are abreast of current community activities, and use these gatherings as an opportunity to publicize your program. Read magazines and newsletters that are targeted to the disabled, and, if possible, place a small ad about your program in these publications. For example, *Careers & the Handicapped* (44 Broadway, Greenlawn, NY 11740; [516] 261-8899) is a magazine that connects businesses with disabled college students and young professionals. Another great resource is the Job Accommodation Network (809 Allen Hall, P.O. Box 6123, West Virginia University, Morgantown, WV 26506; [800] 526-7234). Their database has over twenty thousand ideas for accommodating the disabled in a work area.

I located a television and VCR repair shop in Long Beach, California, that employed kidney dialysis patients. They had five technicians sitting at a test-and-repair workstation repairing electronic entertainment equipment. As they worked, two of the five employees were having their blood cleaned with a portable hemodialysis machine. Self-care and self-reliance are important goals for many disabled persons.

You could actually set up a network of handicapped persons who serve one another's daily household needs. One entrepreneur I know offers a shopping service for the disabled, using other disabled individuals whenever possible. The service purchases groceries, picks up laundry and dry cleaning, and runs errands for a minimal fee. The merchants give this entrepreneur a quantity discount for his patronage. His service has become so popular that the work load now requires three assistants six days a week to meet the demand.

Wouldn't it feel great to be able to help disabled individuals find a worthwhile career opportunity?

RESOURCES

Goodwill Industries of America
9200 Wisconsin Ave.
Bethesda, MD 20814
(301) 530-6500

International Center for the Disabled (ICD)
340 E. 24th
New York, NY 10010
(212) 679-0100

Just One Break
373 Park Ave. S.
New York, NY 10016
(212) 725-2500

Independent Living
Equal Opportunity Publications
44 Broadway
Greenlawn, NY 11740
(516) 261-8917

Disability Studies Quarterly
Brandeis University
Box 9110
Waltham, MA 02254-9110
(617) 736-2644

Worklife
President's Committee on Employment of the Handicapped
Superintendent of Documents 04B
Government Printing Office
Washington, DC 20401
(202) 653-5044

EMPLOYING THE HANDICAPPED LAUNCH CHECKLIST

- ☐ Form a corporation or limited partnership.
- ☐ Open a bank account.
- ☐ Order business cards, stationery, and brochures.
- ☐ File a DBA with local newspaper if you do not incorporate.
- ☐ Obtain city business license if required.
- ☐ Have attorney draft subcontractor agreement.
- ☐ Obtain an IRS tax identification number.
- ☐ Check with your insurance agent about obtaining appropriate insurance coverage.
- ☐ Purchase mailing list from list broker and contact subcontractor candidates.
- ☐ Distribute brochures.
- ☐ Sign up subcontractors and monitor production.
- ☐ Train subcontractors to perform desired service.
- ☐ Write a business plan. Incorporate the knowledge gained from work accomplished on your checklist.

41

Computerized Shopping Service

How many times have you wanted to buy someone a gift but did not know shirt size, waist size, dress size, shoe size, or color preference? This idea for a computerized shopping service is similar to the computerized department store bridal registry, where a bride-to-be registers her china, silver, crystal, and linen selections to assist those wishing to purchase wedding gifts for her and her fiance. Unlike the bridal registry, in this business you are an independent businessperson in a partnership with a shopping center or local department stores.

You input each customer's name, address, and ten to fifteen items of personal information such as clothing sizes, personal and home fashion color schemes, even perhaps most-wished-for gifts into your personal computer in a shopping center or mall location. When a customer's relative, friend, or business associate wants to buy the customer a gift, the person comes to you to access the gift information in your database. For a fee, you provide participating stores a printed copy of your database on a weekly basis.

Keep your start-up costs low by inviting a computer store (preferably one located in the mall or very close by) to provide you with a personal computer, software program, and printer. Offer to place a sign on the computer stating that it was provided by that store. Perhaps one of the questions asked of each participant would be "What type of computer would you like to own and/or do you need any software packages for your computer?" The computer store should love the idea, since you will be in such a highly visible location and will be collecting leads all day long while advertising the store and its merchandise at no out-of-pocket expense except for the use of the firm's equipment.

The computer store owner will still carry the hardware on his or her inventory, since the store still owns the computer. If you already have a personal computer and printer, you're already in business. You should be able to find a number of existing programs that you can readily adapt to your needs.

Next, find a location for your business in a busy mall, preferably in an area with heavy foot traffic. Expect to pay up to $250 weekly for a small space in the middle of the mall, with the rent rising to $500 per week during the holiday seasons. Along with your computer, printer, and diskettes, you'll need a desk or table, a storage bin for hard copies of each customer's data, and at least two chairs. Your personal computer and printer should be on a workstation with wheels so that each evening you may move it to secure it.

Your signage should draw customers to your desk, which should also have your business cards and brochures describing your shopping service, as well as fliers from your partner stores. Before hanging your shingle, check with your city government about obtaining a business license and make sure you are in compliance with any other requirements specific to your type of business.

So how do you make money? There are many potential revenue sources. You can charge each retail store a flat "membership" fee of $50 to $100 per week. If there are twenty-five stores, you would earn $1,250 to $2,500 per week. Each paying store would be entitled to a weekly copy of the computerized list. You could charge the person inquiring about gift ideas $2 for accessing your computer. You could also sell the list to catalog marketers and merchants who want to know the specific needs of prospective customers. Each of these agreements should be in writing, in the form of either a contract or a purchase order.

Shopping mall advertisements and retail store advertisements could include a small coupon for your service that asks for the same information you routinely program into your computer. The customer may either mail it in or drop it off to you the next time he or she is in the mall. The more you get the retail stores involved, the greater the use of your program. Merchants should encourage their customers to fill out your questionnaire in their stores; you pick up the completed forms once a week when you deliver your partners' (the stores') weekly printouts. Consider providing each store with a counter card advertisement as a point-of-purchase display.

After a period of time, your service will become known to the mall and its retail tenants. In addition to selling more products, your service will encourage more people to shop at their mall, because other malls won't have the computerized gift information available. Moreover, exchanges should decrease dramatically as people get into the habit of buying their friends and relatives clothing that fits properly in appropriate color choices, as well as other gifts that are sure to please.

You may want to expand your basic information-gathering business into a shopping service. Busy business executives, people who hate to shop, those who are ill, shut-ins, and other reluctant shoppers could phone in for personal information, then have you pick the gifts out and have them gift wrapped for pickup or delivery. You could charge a 10 percent shopping fee plus a delivery charge of $5 to $10 depending upon the destination. Many merchants in the shopping center should gladly give you a 10 percent discount because they should recognize that your potential volume of purchases is high and that you are partners. That will give you a 20 percent profit margin plus the profit on deliveries. Once your business has developed to this point, you'll need to hire a part-time person to assist you.

All of the stores that you buy from should be willing to allow you to place your brochures on their counters. Also, you will want to distribute your brochures to physicians, attorneys, accountants, dentists, and other professionals in your area, since they often have difficulty finding enough time to shop. Make it easy for them while earning profits for yourself.

RESOURCES

National Retail Merchants Association
100 W. 31st St.
New York, NY 10001
(212) 244-8780

Online Today
5000 Arlington Center Blvd.
Columbus, OH 43220
(614) 457-8600

COMPUTERIZED SHOPPING SERVICE
LAUNCH CHECKLIST

☐ Form a company.

☐ Open a checking account.

☐ Visit local IRS office to obtain an IRS tax identification number.

☐ Obtain city business license if required.

☐ Order business cards, stationery, and simple brochure from a local printer.

☐ Have attorney draft merchant participation agreement.

☐ File DBA with local newspaper.

☐ Establish phone-answering service or buy an answering machine. If you are working a booth or space in a shopping mall, you won't be home to answer the phone.

☐ Check with owner of local computer store to arrange for hardware and software requirements.

☐ Distribute brochures to local professionals.

☐ Have sign lettered by local sign shop, or use art type to make your own if capital is limited.

☐ Meet with shopping center managers and store owners in shopping malls to negotiate participation agreement.

☐ Write a business plan. Incorporate the knowledge gained from work accomplished on your checklist.

42

Home-Appliance Repair

Everything breaks down sooner or later. Unfortunately most things break down when you either cannot afford to fix them or desperately need them. The only time my television ever breaks down is just before the Super Bowl or World Series playoffs. My refrigerator breaks down on the hottest day of summer, and my radio doesn't work during the one-and-only earthquake that I've ever experienced. And does the dishwasher ever break down unless you have a houseful of guests? Adding insult to injury, these things always break down on Saturday night when the only repairman available is going to charge you five times the normal labor rate. Of course, after you agree to pay this holdup man his exorbitant rate, he has to come back on Monday because he doesn't have the required parts with him. The Amish may have the right idea, since they don't have to worry about electrical appliances breaking down.

If you don't live in an Amish community, I have a great idea for you. Provide a preventive maintenance and emergency home physical plant and appliance repair service for homeowners. Homeowners would pay a flat monthly fee for coverage of the basic items, but coverage of additional items, such as a pool or spa, would require an initial evaluation fee of $25 to $50 and would also increase the monthly fee.

Working out of your house to keep your start-up expenses to a minimum, you can begin this business with very little money, and your ongoing costs should be almost totally administrative. Simply negotiate discounted hourly service rates with a television repair shop; refrigerator repair technician; furnace, water heater, and air-conditioning repairperson; small-appliance repair shop; and dishwasher repair service. As you like, you can add

242

personal computers, VCRs, stereo systems, and lawn care equipment to your homeowner maintenance and repair contract.

Offer homeowners a basic preventive maintenance agreement for $55 per month. (This figure is used for discussion purposes. Obviously, you must calculate your costs for repairpeople and build in a profit for yourself.) For this one low monthly payment, you would provide periodic maintenance service on a scheduled basis. Your heating and air-conditioning specialist would replace the air filter, clean the furnace, and make minor adjustments as required. Your television repairperson would make routine adjustments and replace defective parts. The refrigerator repairperson would replace coolant, clean and tune the machine if required, and so on. If equipment breaks down, you agree to dispatch a serviceperson at no additional cost, although you will bill for parts (at list price). The customer would have to pay for replacement of equipment, so if a new water heater is needed, the customer would have to pay for it, along with any installation costs.

Your task is to negotiate good agreements with the service personnel and sell the program to homeowners. First, contact an attorney to draft a standard homeowner agreement outlining your program and policies. Your lawyer should also draft a basic agreement for your service vendors, which may need modification depending upon the particular service and maintenance schedule. Marketing your business is relatively straightforward. Develop a one-page, one-color descriptive brochure for distribution to real estate offices, condominium owners, apartment complexes, and individual homeowners. Since there are homes and homeowners everywhere, the sky's the limit.

At this point, you're probably saying, "OK, Chuck, but how much money can I make?" Each month a different serviceperson would spend one-half to one hour at each of your customer's homes. Rather than charging the homeowner for the call, the serviceperson would bill you $25 to $35 per call. A serviceperson who makes seven calls per day will earn between $175 and $245 per day plus profits from the purchase of parts. Each serviceperson will have a guaranteed revenue stream with no sales or scheduling expenses and is positioned to sell his or her products, whether refrigerators, televisions, VCRs, or water heaters. This is not a small market! Dealerscope Merchandising's *Merchandising* reports that manufacturers ship over fifty-one million major appliances every year.

You will earn $20 per month per customer plus a 10 percent parts profit and a 10 percent commission on all equipment replacement. For each seven hours billed, you will earn $140. That is $840 per six-day week, or over $43,680 per year, minus any vacation time. If you double the number of hours billed, you will earn nearly $87,360 per year!

RESOURCES

National Appliance Service Association
406 W. 34th St., Ste. 628
Kansas City, MO 64111
(816) 753-0210

Appliance Service News
110 W. St. Charles Rd.
P.O. Box 789
Lombard, IL 60148
(708) 932-9550

HOME-APPLIANCE REPAIR BUSINESS LAUNCH CHECKLIST

☐ Meet with attorney to form a corporation and draft home-owner and vendor agreements.
☐ Open a bank account.
☐ Order business cards, stationery, and brochures.
☐ Obtain city business license if required.
☐ Obtain an IRS tax identification number from local IRS office.
☐ Check with your insurance agent about appropriate coverage.
☐ Set up workbench repair area in your garage if you are going to do your own work.

☐ Contact local repair shops and negotiate discounted rates for parts and service.

☐ Distribute brochure to homeowners and real estate offices throughout your community. Also provide participating subcontractors an ample supply for their sales counters.

☐ Write a business plan. Incorporate the knowledge gained from work accomplished on your checklist.

PART III
BUSINESS TACTICS

43

Network Marketing

In 1989 *Advertising Age* predicted that corporations would begin transferring as much as 40 percent of their budgets for mass media campaigns to "point-of-purchase" marketing efforts—that is, selling their products directly to the consumer without the use of middlemen. The only mistake *Advertising Age* made was being too conservative. Recent estimates indicate that 60 percent of all manufacturers and marketers now want to spend their promotional dollars as close as possible to the consumer.

One of the means they have recently discovered for this point-of-purchase marketing is network marketing, or, as it has traditionally been known, multilevel marketing (MLM). An MLM company allows you to earn overrides on the sales made by distributors you've enlisted to sell your company's products as well as to earn commissions on products you sell yourself. To say that MLM has just been discovered is a little ironic, since it has been knocking around the American economy for nearly half a century, and it has been a power in the world economy for more than two decades. Companies such as Amway, Shaklee, and Mary Kay have become billion-dollar industries promoting their products through MLM channels.

However, it is only in the past five years that MLM has really come into its own, while remaining a well-kept secret of the several million Americans making money this way. Few people know that last year the Water Quality Association reported that two out of every three water filters sold in America were sold by MLM companies. MCI sold nearly half its residential customers through Amway, while Sprint sold more than 50 percent of its residential long-distance customers through Network 2000, a network marketing company. A. L. Williams, an MLM marketer of insurance, sells more policies each year than the next two largest American insurance companies combined, reporting $500 million in profits last year!

What accounts for the tremendous effectiveness and recent triumph of this form of marketing? First, MLM has recently found the technological support required to make it successful. Jenkon Data Systems, Inc., the largest supplier of computer programming and support for MLM companies, began business in 1980. Computer support is essential to make MLM a no-hassle opportunity for the independent distributors who run MLM businesses out of their homes on a part-time basis.

A second reason for the success of MLM is the recent explosion of entrepreneurial activity in America and throughout the world. While many studies predicted that more than 80 percent of the American work force would be employed by megacorporations by the year 1990, just the opposite is true. In fact, the most frequently cited goal of graduating MBAs in 1990 was *not* to go to work for a corporation, but to get into some form of entrepreneurial operation.

This independence in the private sector has been mirrored in the public/political sector by the recent collapse of socialism. When Avenues Communication, a firm specializing in MLM corporate projects, recently interviewed leaders in Solidarity about what they had been able to learn from American "big business," the leaders replied, "Practically nothing. It is the small business entrepreneur who is teaching us the most." In fact, the word for entrepreneur in Polish is *entrepreneur*, since the use of the word in Poland is so recent that it has no Polish equivalent!

To further fan the fires of MLM's success, Milton Friedman, the University of Chicago professor emeritus and Nobel Laureate in economics, recently said that the greatest economic need of most Americans is for cottage industries: businesses they can run out of their homes, on their own time, conforming to their own schedules; businesses that do not depend on the goodwill of others; businesses that can increase the discretionary income of the average worker, but not at the expense of his or her family life. Such cottage industries are especially valuable in times of recession or other economic uncertainty.

As important as any other element in the success of network marketing is what *Advertising Age* predicted: manufacturers are looking for a way to spend advertising dollars as close to the point of sale as possible. For this reason companies such as Broadcast International have become successful in the past few years, beaming ads by satellite into the aisles where shoppers stop, telling people to buy this soup or that bread when they can reach out and act on the ad right then and there.

That's what network marketing does: it provides a one-on-one sales presentation to potential customers right at the point of sale. A person who wants to buy doesn't have to turn off the TV and go to the market, dial an 800 number, or mail anything in. All the customer has to do is say yes. And the customer is likely to say yes, because MLM distributors are usually among the most enthusiastic and committed sales professionals in the marketplace today.

Successful MLM companies should have several characteristics:

- Charismatic products that need a story to be told for them to be successfully marketed.
- Technical support and computer support that make it possible for relatively inexperienced distributors to capitalize upon their enthusiasm.
- Low start-up costs—MLMs traditionally have provided a minimum investment, minimum risk, and maximum potential.
- Mainstream affiliation—MLM distributors look for solid product affiliations—companies, products, or projects they recognize that provide support, integrity, and substantiation for their own efforts.
- Training for its distributors—since many MLMers are part-time people with little experience in business or sales, a successful MLM company must provide effective training programs.
- Good timing—the product and the opportunity must be right for the times. Amway made a fortune in soap; Shaklee did extraordinarily well in vitamins; Mary Kay made a killing in cosmetics. But what is the product of today . . . and of the future?

What can happen when you put all these together in the right company? Six-figure incomes are not uncommon, and the fast-tracking companies frequently produce distributors earning $30,000 to $40,000 a month!

So, if you decide to enter network marketing, which MLM company do you choose? Several satisfy these criteria. One that is especially interesting is Softron International (5220 Edison, Chino, CA 91710; [714] 628-0644). Not only does Softron seem to fulfill the criteria for a successful network marketing company, but its products are particularly well suited for the times. All you have to do is open a marketing publication to learn that one of the trends in goods and services expected to explode over the next few years is environmental products. Softron's Airtron is a revolutionary air filter that looks more like a designer potted plant. Air is drawn through the soil of the plant, where a group of microbes devours toxins. Softron also markets other environmentally sensitive products, including magnetic water and fuel conditioners and a remarkable product called "HydroSoil," which promotes water conservation when mixed with the soil in potted plants, lawns, gardens, and agricultural fields.

Obviously, Softron is not the only MLM opportunity out there, but it is one of the best.

RESOURCES

Multi-Level Marketing Association
119 Stanford
Irvine, CA 92715
(714) 854-5488

Direct Marketing
224 Seventh St.
Garden City, NY 11530
(516) 746-6700

44

Motivation

Two essential components in a successful business venture are motivation and enthusiasm. One of the best anecdotes about motivation is the story of the workers at Carnegie Steel. The night shift wrote their night's production on the floor when the shift ended. The day shift saw the production figure and set about to improve on it. At the end of their shift, they scratched out the night shift's number and wrote their better number on the floor. The night shift responded, and the competition carried on, with the obvious consequences for production output.

The story may not be literally true, but the message is on target. Motivation affects performance. It's easy to recognize that a motivated employee accomplishes more. A group of motivated people, such as a department or a company, accomplishes more. Therefore, the view your staff members hold about their work has significant consequences for you, the owner. Let's spend some time looking at motivation.

THE HAWTHORNE EFFECT

In 1927 Elton Mayo undertook one of the first modern studies of work behavior as it relates to productivity. The study took place with workers at the Hawthorne Works of the Western Electric Company in what is now Cicero, Illinois. Looking for ways to explain levels of productivity, Mayo's experiments actually demonstrated the effects of motivation. The results became known as the "Hawthorne effect."

Mayo tested the effects of several variables on productivity. Wages, rest periods, hours, degree of supervision, lighting, and temperature were among the factors tested. The results were consistently the same. No matter how these factors were varied, productivity went up. The most important result was that the experiment created an esprit de corps that was critically tied to the increased productivity. The "environmental" variables— changes in hours and wages, etc.—faded in importance in comparison to the social and psychological influences—human interest and attention—given to the workers at the Hawthorne Works. The human variable raised the level of motivation and, consequently, the level of productivity.

The significant point here is that human beings react to other human beings. Your employees, be they two or two hundred, will react to you. The interest you take in your employees, and the attention you pay to them, will have more to do with their level of motivation than anything else will. Level of motivation has more to do with the level of accomplishment than anything else. Understanding your employees, what makes them "turn on" or "turn off" to the work process, is key to being able to get things done through them. Let's consider how certain theories view the role of your influence on the level of employee motivation.

MASLOW

In his 1954 book, *Motivation & Personality*, Abraham H. Maslow developed a theory of motivation, which he described in terms of a hierarchy of needs. Generally, the hierarchy means that people are motivated by the lower-level needs until these are satisfied, then they are motivated by higher-level needs. Consider Maslow's hierarchy, presented here in ascending order, in terms of the work situation.

Physiological Needs

The physiological needs are for food, drink, sex, and sleep. If these needs are not satisfied, the employee will not be motivated. For example, if the salary earned is insufficient to provide for physiological needs, the employee's first concern will be to find ways to "earn" more. This may take the form of moonlighting, job hopping, or theft from the company.

While you cannot, and indeed should not, know the personal circumstances of every employee, be aware of whether or not the salary structure generally seems adequate to the majority of your employees. Believe me, you'll know, because they will let you know. If it is not, there is little value in trying to improve performance markedly. You had better consider whether your salary schedule has to be adjusted. This may mean that you must undertake a formal salary survey.

Safety

Stability, freedom from fear, structure, and order are the "safety" needs. At this level, your influence starts to be more noticeable. An orderly work environment, an attitude of purpose and commitment on your part, a reasonable show of tolerance rather than flashing the sword are the ways you influence the level of motivation associated with the safety needs.

Belongingness and Love

The presence of family and friends satisfies the need for belongingness and love. In the business context, a small amount of effort in showing individuals or groups that what they do is needed and valued by the company goes a long way. Employees need to know that they are part of the team, that their jobs are important to the overall company's ability to function.

Esteem

Self-confidence, respect for others, usefulness, and competence are the needs at the next level of Maslow's hierarchy. Showing appreciation for a job well done is key. Take an employee to lunch, or call a staff meeting to single out an employee who has done something well. Show some recognition, and you will build esteem among the members of your entrepreneurial team. Greater self-respect raises the prospects for respecting others, which must exist if people are to function as a team.

Self-Actualization

Growing to meet one's potential is the last and highest level of need in the hierarchy. This is the area of greatest influence for you as an owner. If an employee performs well consistently and wants to do more, give the employee a chance to do more. It will be necessary for you to help your employee assess potential. It will motivate your employee if he or she believes that you will provide the opportunity to develop that potential . . . even if it means that you may "lose" the employee to another department in your company.

Entrepreneurs must effectively apply the hierarchy of needs that Maslow set forth. Understanding the hierarchy and applying the concepts to your management situation can only improve your relationship with your employees and positively affect your bottom line.

McGREGOR

In *The Human Side of Enterprise*, Douglas McGregor discusses how managers view workers (not necessarily how they are). He describes two basic sets of beliefs, which he calls Theory X and Theory Y. A manager or entrepreneur who adheres to Theory X believes that the average employee inherently dislikes work; must be punished, controlled, directed toward work objectives; and prefers to be told what to do. An entrepreneur who takes this view is more likely to be autocratic. There is little room for acknowledging the basic worth of the individual employee and little hope that the hierarchy of needs will be met.

Someone who adopts Theory Y, on the other hand, believes that the average employee:

- Finds effort at work as natural as effort at play.
- Wills self-control, works toward objectives, and is committed.
- Enjoys the rewards of achievement, which themselves regenerate commitment.
- Has the capacity to exercise the imagination—is creative in finding solutions to problems, is more broad than narrow in thinking.

An entrepreneur who takes the Theory Y view is more likely to be participative, seeking the contribution that individuals can make to improving the work process. This kind of entrepreneur is more likely to be a team builder and will have a more highly motivated group of people as a result.

On any given day, of course, people differ. At various points in time, the attributes of both theories will apply to all entrepreneurs. Of significance are the attributes that apply to an entrepreneur over time. If you take the fundamental view that people have needs and abilities, you will find that they can be motivated by organizational objectives and will be able to achieve them.

COMMON SENSE

Let's put what you do as a business owner in terms of the dictates of common sense:

Need: People want to know what is expected of them.
Action: Tell them.

Need: People want to achieve.
Action: Give them goals and a chance.

Need: People want to be noticed.
Action: Pay attention to them.

Need: People want to believe.
Action: Give them a mission.

Need: People want to be appreciated.
Action: Thank them.

Need: People want to care.
Action: Care, and they will.

There are a few additional points that can help you create and maintain a high level of motivation among your employees. They are basic and can be applied naturally.

- A sincere "thanks" is worth a bunch of motivational speeches.
- Reprimands may sometimes be warranted. Don't overuse them, but don't be afraid to use them.

- A compliment is standard, as well as an expression of appreciation. With most people, saying "well done" will result in more opportunities to say "well done."
- A motivated employee is terrific. Build a team of motivated employees.
- A winning team consists of individual winners.

Winning companies are made up of motivated people. They desire to do well, are rewarded for doing well, and will continue to do well if they continue to be motivated. After all, it's fun to win.

45

Organizational Structure

Organizational planning will help you manage your new venture better. Creating and maintaining the proper organization is indeed a management skill you will want to develop. The organizational structure is a means to "running your company." It serves as a delivery system.

Different organizational structures serve different purposes. What can be very good for one company can be entirely inappropriate for another. The job of the entrepreneur is to blend purpose, function, and resources (management and employees) in the best way to deliver the service or product to the market in the most effective manner. The organization serves the operating needs of the company. ("Operating" here refers broadly to manufacturing, marketing, distribution, and so forth.)

Although it may seem premature to you when you are just starting a new business, think for a moment about your company and what the formal organization should be designed to do. These are the primary functions of the organization for your company—as a matter of fact, for any company:

- Carry out the mission of your company.
- Deliver your product or service to the market.
- Allow people to use and develop their capabilities and talents.
- Facilitate productivity.
- Assign financial responsibility, authority, and accountability. Lack of operating capital is the number two reason for corporate bankruptcies.
- Minimize confusion and conflict among the various functional interrelationships.
- Facilitate communication among the various units in your company. Poor management is the number one cause of corporate bankruptcies.

- Build pride of ownership in the work process.
- Help your company make a profit. Insufficient profits is the number three cause of corporate bankruptcies.

While the functions are common to all organizations, no common organizational design fits all companies. Let's consider some examples of different structures that are appropriate for the kind of business the company is in.

FUNCTIONAL ORGANIZATION

One type of structure is based on the major functions performed in the company. Management and employee resources are clustered around these functions. An example would be a burglar alarm business that has three major divisions (designating the major functions): Systems Sales, Installation, and Consulting Services. These divisions, of course, report to a chief executive officer. Labor and management expertise are assigned according to function.

GEOGRAPHIC ORGANIZATION

Companies that have operations distributed over a large geographic area may benefit from a geographic organization. Management and support functions are distributed into geographic centers. An appropriate business for this structure might be a large national retailing company, such as a franchise for the senior-citizen business. The geographic area covered is the United States. The entire area is divided into regions, with senior line managers and employees who are responsible for the individual retail stores in cities assigned to each region. The regions report to company headquarters.

PRODUCT ORGANIZATION

Management and staff resources may also be assigned to major product lines. A cooperative purchasing service comes to mind here. The major divisions are Merchant Participants, Customers, and Financing. In this instance, financing refers to the process of enabling buyers to borrow money so they can make the purchase; in other words, the product is a financing service.

CUSTOMER SEGMENT ORGANIZATION

A company may be organized around the major market (customer) segments that it serves. An example would be a security guard business with major divisions established according to basic customer groups: banking, hospitals, corporate clients, construction, special events, and so on. Because the financial requirements of the groups are distinctive and, in some cases, dramatically different, the structure recognizes the customer segments. Management and employees specialize according to the segment served.

PROCESS ORGANIZATION

Major divisions in a process organization recognize the key stages in a process. An example is a water conservation company that has these divisions: Fixtures (devices like faucets and water-reduction toilets), Chemicals (such as polymers), Installation, and Distribution. Getting the product from the manufacturer to the market involves passing through major steps, each of which requires different management and labor skills. The structure accommodates the process and makes the most of everyone's talents.

MATRIX ORGANIZATION

Other structures come into and go out of vogue. For instance, a few years ago the "matrix" organization was quite popular. In this structure, management and employees are grouped according to professional specialty, then allocated to operating units on a "dotted-line" basis. In other words, employees report to a manager in their specialty and also (along a "dotted line") to a manager of the project they are currently working on. An illustration would be a centralized research group whose time and efforts are allocated to major product divisions. Individual members of the research group are assigned to the individual product divisions (dotted-line reporting) for support but continue to be accountable to the research group management (solid-line reporting).

This kind of structure can create some serious internal difficulties. An individual member of the research group effectively has two masters—the research manager and the product manager. There can be turf battles over which manager's judgment prevails when disputes arise. Accounting for the cost of the research resource can be confusing when an individual or unit in the research group serves more than one product division. And what if the product division does not like the "quality" of the research? Because the matrix organization in many instances caused more problems than it solved, it has recently been abandoned by many companies.

FLOW OF DIRECTION AND COMMUNICATION

A version of the conventional organization that generally does not function well is the "top-down" structure, shown in the illustration. In this kind of company, management makes all decisions unilaterally and passes them down through the organization. This may work well in a small entrepreneurial business, but it will not work well in larger organizations. The issues are too many and too complex for one or two at the top to make all the decisions.

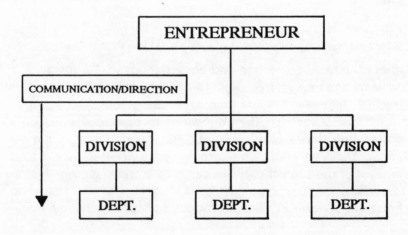

Although the next "org chart" looks the same, the nature of the management process is significantly different. Note that communication and direction flow two ways: up and down. Participation means that lower levels of management have input into decisions made at the higher level. This allows the entrepreneur to take advantage of subordinates' knowledge, improving the prospects for sound decisions at each organizational level.

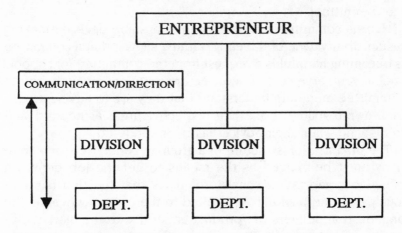

For this structure to function well, some additional characteristics need to be present:

- Within each unit (department, division), someone must be in charge—a boss—and ultimately responsible for decisions and unit performance.
- Responsibility must be appropriately assigned to each unit (department or division) according to the function that unit performs. Marketing, for example, must not be assigned the responsibility for quality control in the manufacturing units. Of course, we all recognize the need to wear several hats during the "launch" phase of a new business.
- When a manager assigns responsibility, he or she must also grant authority to make the necessary decisions. This is a particularly bitter pill for many entrepreneurs to swallow, but it must be taken.
- Accountability for decisions made must be tied to the authority to make decisions.

COMMITTEES

A discussion of organization also calls to mind the committee. There are really only two kinds of committees: the helpful committee and the harmful committee.

Helpful committees provide advice and counsel to the entrepreneur and are also a vehicle for communication in your company (assuming, of course, that several areas are represented on the committee).

Harmful committees are assigned or assume decision-making responsibility. One of the early warning signals that a committee is becoming harmful is a request from the committee for support staff. If you serve on a committee or create one, make sure the committee members understand that they are to advise, to use their own resources from their respective areas as needed, and to disband when their advice has been rendered.

The organization structure of a group, a committee, or a company must be viewed as the means to get the job done. An effective organization consists of parts that function harmoniously and purposefully. As applied to the company overall, the organization delivers the product or service to the market efficiently and at a profit. Regardless of the size of the group you manage, your company's organization must have the attributes described in this chapter in order to serve you and your company well.

SUCCESSION PLANNING

Related to the subject of organization is succession planning. Here's a mixed bag of observations on that topic:

- Succession planning is critical to an orderly evolution of the organization over time.
- It can be done simply.
- It must be done regularly.
- It is sometimes ignored.
- It is frequently made complicated, even esoteric.
- It can lose purpose if the succession planners become so involved in the process that they lose sight of the objective.

You should have a succession plan for your company. Use a form to develop succession candidates for the employees who report to you. Three candidates, identified in order of preference, will be adequate most of the time. Consider that the candidates can be drawn from other units within the company, or even from other companies if appropriate. Also, if some of your staff members have highly specialized skills, you may want to consider succession planning for them.

Keep your succession-planning process simple and the paperwork at a minimum, but remember to update your plan regularly. Some of the businesses described in this book, such as the security guard, dinner delivery, and valet parking businesses, have a comparatively high turnover rate. When employee changes do occur, you will manage them better if you have planned for them.

46

Conclusion

I hope that one of the businesses in this book will provide you with the vehicle that you need to find financial freedom. Do not despair if none of them quite matches your needs. The concepts and practical applications are transferable to hundreds of businesses. Throughout my life, as I have gone from investment to investment, I am ever mindful of the need to make stone soup.

When you first started to read *How to Get Rich*, you may have been looking for a way to improve your chances at business success. In chapter after chapter you have read the steps an entrepreneur needs to take a concept from the drawing board to the boardroom. Now that you know how it's done, the ball is in your court. Write to me and let me know how you are doing. Good luck!

Charles R. Whitlock
2899 Agoura Rd., Ste. 316
Westlake Village, CA 91361